LOOKING FORWARD

Franklin D. Roosevelt

A TOUCHSTONE BOOK
Published by Simon & Schuster
New York   London   Toronto   Sydney

 Touchstone
A Division of Simon & Schuster, Inc.
1230 Avenue of the Americas
New York, NY 10020

This Touchstone trade paperback edition January 2009

TOUCHSTONE and colophon are registered trademarks of Simon & Schuster, Inc.

For information about special discounts for bulk purchases,
please contact Simon & Schuster Special Sales at
1-800-456-6798 or business@simonandschuster.com.

Designed by Renata Di Biase

Manufactured in the United States of America

10   9   8   7   6   5   4   3   2

The Library of Congress has cataloged the John Day edition as follows:
Roosevelt, Franklin D. (Franklin Delano), 1882–1945.
    Looking forward / by Franklin D. Roosevelt.
        p.   cm.
    "First printing, March 1933 . . . Fourth printing, March 1933."
    Has index.
        1. United States—Economic policy—1933–1945.   2. United
States—Economic conditions—1918–1945.   3. United States—
Social conditions—1933–1945.   4. United States—Politics and
government—1933–1945.   I. Title.
E743 .R664   33-23948

ISBN-13: 978-1-4391-4869-3
ISBN-10:   1-4391-4869-4

CONTENTS

INTRODUCTION

THIS IS ESSENTIALLY a compilation from many articles written and speeches made prior to March 1, 1933. I have added parts which bind the material together as a whole.

In the comments to follow I speak not of politics but of government, not of parties but of universal principles. They are not political except in that large sense in which a great American once expressed a definition of politics—that nothing in all human life is foreign to the science of politics.

The quality of national politics, viewed as a science which is capable of affecting for the better the lives of the average man and woman in America, is the concern of national leadership—particularly in such years as these when the hand of discouragement has fallen upon us, when it seems that things are in a rut, fixed, settled, that the world has grown old and tired and very much out of joint. That is the mood of depression, of dire and weary depression which, if the quality of our political leadership is right, should vanish so utterly that it will be difficult to reconstruct the mood.

Everything tells us that such a philosophy of futility is wrong. America is new. It is in the process of change and development. It has the great potentialities of youth. But youth can batter itself to death against the stone wall of political and governmental ineptitude.

That our government has been created by ourselves, that its policies and therefore many of its detailed acts have been ordered by us, is obvious. It is just as true that our interest in government is a self-interest, though it cannot be called selfish, for when we secure an act of government which is helpful to ourselves it should be helpful to all men. Until we look about us we are likely to forget how hard people have worked for the privilege of government.

Good government should maintain the balance where every individual may have a place if he will take it, where every individual may find safety if he wishes it, where every individual may attain such power as his ability permits, consistent with his assuming the accompanying responsibility.

The achievement of good government is therefore a long, slow task. Nothing is more striking than the simple innocence of the men who insist whenever an objective is present, on the prompt production of a patent scheme guaranteed to produce a result.

Human endeavor is not so simple as that. Government includes the art of formulating policies and using the political technique to attain so much of them as will receive general support; persuading, leading, sacrificing, teaching always, because perhaps the greatest duty of statesmanship is to educate.

We must build toward the time when a major depression cannot occur again; and if this means sacrificing the easy profits of inflationist booms, then let them go—and good riddance.

Our recent experiences with speculation have distorted the perspective of many minds. A whole generation had gone mad over that word cooperation; there had been many conferences of this and of that industry, trade papers, codes of ethics, red-fire and "pep talks"—all aimed to build up sales and more production. What had been lacking was the kind of planning which would prevent and not stimulate overproduction. It is natural that in the minds of many, first one plan of action and then another seemed of paramount importance. It is natural that the scrapping of industries, and even institutions which seemed the bulwarks of our strength, bewildered even those who had heretofore been able to find in past history practical suggestions for present action. It would be natural, when such experience seemed to contribute nothing, that the great social phenomenon of this depression would produce disorderly manifestations. Yet wild radicalism has made few converts, and the greatest tribute I can pay my countrymen is that in these days of crushing want, there persists an orderly and hopeful spirit on the part of the millions of our people who have suffered so much. To fail to offer them a new chance is not only to betray their hopes but to misunderstand their patience.

To meet by reaction that danger of radicalism is to invite disaster. It is a challenge, a provocation. The way to meet that danger is to offer a workable program of reconstruction. This, and this only, is a proper protection against blind reaction on the one hand and improvised hit-or-miss, irresponsible opportunism on the other.

My party is neither new nor untried. My national leadership of it is new to the extent that within the party it legally dates, if that term may be used, from the moment its delegates, in convention assembled, nominated me for the Presidency. But a new man in that leadership should not mean an untried concept of policies; they must be firmly rooted in the governmental experience of the past.

Federalism, as Woodrow Wilson so wisely put it, was a group "possessed of unity and informed by a conscious solidarity of interest." It was Jefferson's purpose to teach the country that the solidarity of Federalism was only a partial one, that it represented only a minority of the people and that to build a great nation the interests of all groups in every part must be considered. He has been called a politician because he devoted years to the building of a political party. But his labor was in itself a definite and practical contribution to the unification of all parts of the country in support of common principles. When people carelessly or snobbishly deride political parties, they overlook the fact that the party system of government is one of the greatest methods of unification and of teaching people to think in common terms of our civilization.

We have in our own history three men who chiefly stand

out for the universality of their interest and of their knowledge—Benjamin Franklin, Thomas Jefferson and Theodore
Roosevelt. All three knew at first hand every cross current
of national and of international life. All three were possessed of a profound culture in the best sense of the word,
and yet all three understood the yearnings and the lack of
opportunity—the hopes and fears of millions of their fellow
beings. All true culture finally comes down to an apprecia-
tion of just that.

And of the three, I think that Jefferson was in many ways
the deepest student—the one with the most inquiring and
diversified intellect and, above all, the one who at all times
looked the farthest into the future, examining the ultimate
effects on humanity of the actions of the present.

Jefferson's methods were usually illustrative of government based upon a universality of interest. I can picture the
weeks on horseback when he was travelling into the different states of the union, slowly and laboriously accumulat-
ing an understanding of the people of his country. He was
not only drinking in the needs of the people in every walk
of life, but he was also giving to them an understanding of
the essential principles of self-government.

Jefferson was so big in mind and spirit that he knew the
average man would understand when he said, "I shall often
go wrong through defective judgment: And when right, I
shall be thought wrong by those whose positions will not
command a view of the whole ground. I ask your support
against the errors of others who may condemn what they
would not, if seen in all the parts."

I shall not speak of an economic life completely planned and regulated. That is as impossible as it is undesirable. I shall speak of the necessity, wherever it is imperative that government interfere to adjust parts of the economic structure of the nation, that there be a real community of interest—not only among the sections of this great country, but among the economic units and the various groups in these units; that there be a common participation in the work of remedial figures, planned on the basis of a shared common life, the low as well as the high. On much of our present plans there is too much disposition to mistake the part for the whole, the head for the body, the captain for the company, the general for the army. I plead not for a class control but for a true concert of interests.

The plans we make during the present emergency, if we plan wisely and rest our structure upon a base sufficiently broad, may show the way to a more permanent safeguarding of our social and economic life, to the end that we may in a large measure avoid the terrible cycle of prosperity crumbling into depression. In this sense I favor economic planning, not for this period alone but for our needs for a long time to come.

If Jefferson could return to our councils he would find that while economic changes of a century have changed the necessary methods of government action, the principles of that action are still wholly his own. He labored for a widespread concert of thought, capable of concert of action, based on a fair and just concert of interests. He labored to bring the scattered farmers, the workers, the business men into a participation in national affairs. This was his purpose and this is the principle upon which the party he founded was based. It should now present itself as an agency of national unity.

Faith in America, faith in our tradition of our personal responsibility, faith in our institutions, faith in ourselves, demands that we recognize the new terms of the old social contract. In this comment I outline my basic conception of these terms, with the confidence that you will follow the action of your new national administration, understanding that its aims and objects arc yours and that our responsibility is mutual.

Hyde Park
March 1, 1933

I

REAPPRAISAL OF VALUES

THE ISSUE OF government has always been whether individual men and women will have to serve some system of government or economics or whether a system of government and economics exists to serve individual men and women.

This question has persistently dominated the discussions of government for many generations. On questions relating to these things men have differed, and from time immemorial it is probable that honest men will continue to differ.

The final word belongs to no man; yet we can still believe in change and progress. Democracy, as Meredith Nicholson has called it, is a quest, a never-ending seeking for these things and striving for them. There are many roads to follow. If we take their course we find there are only two general directions in which they lead. The first is toward government for the benefit of the few, the second is toward government for the benefit of the many.

The growth of the national governments of Europe was a struggle for the development of a centralized force in the nation, strong enough to impose peace upon ruling barons. In many instances the victory of the central government, the creation of a strong central government, was a haven of refuge to the individual. The people preferred the great master far away to the exploitation and cruelty of the smaller master near at hand.

But the creators of national government were perforce ruthless men. They were often cruel in their methods, though they did strive steadily toward something that society needed and very much wanted—a strong central State, able to keep the peace, to stamp out civil war, to put the unruly nobleman in his place and to permit the bulk of individuals to live safely.

The man of ruthless force had his place in developing a pioneer country, just as he did in fixing the power of the central government in the development of the nations. Society paid him well for his services toward its development. When the development among the nations of Europe, however, had been completed, ambition and ruthlessness, having served its term, tended to overstep the mark.

There now came a growing feeling that government was conducted for the benefit of the few who thrived unduly at the expense of all. The people sought a balancing—a limiting force. Gradually there came through town councils, trade guilds, national parliaments, by constitutions and popular participation and control, limitations on arbitrary power. Another factor that tended to limit the power of those who ruled was the rise of the ethical conception that a ruler bore a responsibility for the welfare of his subjects.

The American colonies were born during this struggle. The American Revolution was a turning point in it. After the Revolution the struggle continued and shaped itself into the public life of this country.

There were those who, because they had seen the confusion which attended the years of war for American independence, surrendered to the belief that popular government was essentially dangerous and essentially unworkable. These thinkers were, generally, honest and we cannot deny that their experience had warranted some measure of fear.

The most brilliant, honest and able exponent of this point of view was Hamilton. He was too impatient of slow-moving methods. Fundamentally, he believed that the safety of the Republic lay in the autocratic strength of its government, that the destiny of individuals was to serve that government and that a great and strong group of central institutions, guided by a small group of able and public-spirited citizens, could best direct all government.

But Jefferson, in the summer of 1776, after drafting the Declaration of Independence, turned his mind to the same problem and took a different view. He did not deceive himself with outward forms. Government with him was a means to an end, not an end in itself; it might be either a refuge and a help or a threat and a danger, depending on the circumstances. We find him carefully analyzing the society for which he was to organize a government:

"We have no paupers—the great mass of our population is of laborers, our rich who can live without labor, either manual or professional, being few and of moderate wealth.

Most of the laboring class possess property, cultivate their own lands, have families and from the demands for their labor are enabled to extract from the rich and the competent such prices as enable them to feed abundantly; clothe above mere decency, to labor moderately and raise their families."

These people, he considered, had two sets of rights, those of "personal competency" and those involved in acquiring and possessing property. By "personal competency" he meant the right of free thinking, freedom of forming and expressing opinions and freedom of personal living, each man according to his own lights.

To insure the first set of rights a government must so order its functions as not to interfere with the individual. But even Jefferson realized that the exercise of the property rights must so interfere with the rights of the individual that the government, without whose assistance the property rights could not exist, must intervene, not to destroy individualism but to protect it.

We are familiar with the great political duel which followed; and how Hamilton and his friends, building toward a dominant, centralized power, were at length defeated in the great election of 1800 by Jefferson's party. Out of that duel came the two parties, Republican and Democratic, as we know them today.

So began, in American political life, the new day, the day of the individual against the system, the day in which individualism was made the great watchword in American life. The happiest of economic conditions made that day long and splendid. On the Western frontier land was substantially free. No one who did not shirk the task of earning a living was entirely without opportunity to do so. Depressions could, and did, come and go; but they could not alter the fundamental fact that most of the people lived partly by selling their labor and partly by extracting their livelihood from the soil, so that starvation and dislocation were practically impossible. At the very worst there was always the possibility of climbing into a covered wagon and moving West, where the untilled prairies afforded a haven for men to whom the East did not provide a place.

So great were our natural resources that we could offer this relief not only to our own people but to the distressed of all the world. We could invite immigration from Europe and welcome it with open arms.

When a depression came a new section of land was opened in the West. This became our tradition. So even our temporary misfortune served our manifest destiny.

But a new force was released and a new dream created in the middle of the nineteenth century. The force was what is called the industrial revolution, the advance of steam and machinery and the rise of the forerunners of the modern industrial plant. The dream was that of an economic machine, able to raise the standard of living for everyone; to bring luxury within the reach of the humblest; to annihilate distance by steam power and later by electricity, and to release everyone from the drudgery of the heaviest manual toil.

It was to be expected that the force and the dream would necessarily affect government. Heretofore, government had merely been called upon to produce conditions within which people could live happily, labor peacefully and rest secure. Now it was called upon to aid in the consummation of this new dream. There was, however, a shadow over it. To make the dream real required use of the talents of men of tremendous will and tremendous ambition, since in no other way could the problems of financing and engineering and new development be met.

So manifest were the advantages of the machine age, however, that the United States fearlessly, cheerfully and, I think, rightly accepted the bitter with the sweet. It was thought that no price was too high for the advantages which we could draw from a finished industrial system.

The history of the last half century is accordingly in large measure a history of financial titans, whose methods were not scrutinized with too much care and who were honored in proportion as they produced the results, irrespective of the means they used. The financiers who pushed the railroads to the Pacific, for example, were always ruthless, often wasteful and frequently corrupt, but they did build railroads and we have them today. It has been estimated that the American investor paid for the American railway system more than three times over in the process, but despite this fact the net advantage was to the United States.

As long as we had free land, as long as population was growing by leaps and bounds, as long as our industrial plants were insufficient to supply our own needs, society chose to give the ambitious man free play and unlimited reward, provided only that he produced the economic plant so much desired.

During the period of expansion there was equal economic opportunity for all, and the business of government was not to interfere but to assist in the development of industry. This was done at the request of the business men themselves. The tariff was originally imposed for the purpose of "fostering our infant industry," a phrase which the older among my readers will remember as a political issue not so long ago.

The railroads were subsidized, sometimes by grants of money, oftener by grants of land. Some of the most valuable oil lands in the United States were granted to assist the financing of the railroad which pushed through the Southwest. A nascent merchant marine was assisted by grants of money or by mail subsidies, so that our steam shipping might ply the seven seas. . . .

We do not want the government in business. But we must realize the implications of the past. For while it has been American doctrine that the government must not go into business in competition with private enterprises, still it has been traditional for business to urgently ask the government to put at private disposal all kinds of government assistance.

The same man who says he does not want to see the government interfere in business—and he means it and has plenty of good reasons for saying so—is the first to go to Washington to ask the government for a prohibitory tariff on his product. When things get just bad enough—as they did in 1930—he will go with equal speed to the United States Government and ask for a loan. And the Reconstruction Finance Corporation is the outcome of that.

Each group has sought protection from the government for its own special interests without realizing that the function of government must be to favor no small group at the expense of its duty to protect the rights of personal freedom and of private property of all its citizens.

In retrospect we can see now that the turn of the tide came with the turn of the century. We were reaching our last frontier then; there was no more free land and our industrial combinations had become great uncontrolled and irresponsible units of power within the State.

Clear-sighted men saw with fear the danger that opportunity would no longer be equal; that the growing corporation, like the feudal baron of old, might threaten the economic freedom of individuals to earn a living. In that hour our anti-trust laws were born.

The cry was raised against the great corporations. Theodore Roosevelt, the first great Republican Progressive, fought a Presidential campaign on the issues of "trust busting" and talked freely about malefactors of great wealth. If the government had a policy it was rather to turn the clock back, to destroy the large combinations and to return to the time when every man owned his individual small business. This was impossible. Theodore Roosevelt, abandoning his idea of "trust busting," was forced to work out a difference between "good" trusts and "bad" trusts. The Supreme Court set forth the famous "rule of reason" by which it seems to have meant that a concentration of industrial power was permissible if the method by which it got its power and the use it made of that power was reasonable.

The situation was seen more clearly by Woodrow Wilson, elected in 1912. Where Jefferson had feared the encroachment of political power on the lives of individuals, Wilson knew that the new power was financial. He saw, in the highly centralized economic system, the despot of the twentieth century, on whom great masses of individuals relied for their safety and their livelihood, and whose irresponsibility and greed (if it were not controlled) would reduce them to starvation and penury.

The concentration of financial power had not proceeded as far in 1912 as it has today, but it had grown far enough for Wilson to realize fully its implications. It is interesting now to read his speeches. What is called "radical" today (and I have reason to know whereof I speak) is mild compared to Wilson's Presidential campaign.

"No man can deny," he said, "that the lines of endeavor have more and more narrowed and stiffened; no man who knows anything about the development of industry in this country can have failed to observe that larger kinds of credit are more and more difficult to obtain unless you obtain them upon terms of uniting your efforts with those who already control the industry of the country, and nobody can fail to observe that every man who tries to set himself up in competition with any process of manufacture which has taken place under the control of large combinations of capital will presently find himself either squeezed out or obliged to sell and allow himself to be absorbed."

Had there been no World War—had Wilson been able to devote eight years to domestic instead of international affairs—we might have had a wholly different situation at the present time. However, the then distant roar of European cannon, growing ever louder, forced him to abandon the study of this issue. The problem he saw so clearly is left with us as a legacy; and no one of us of whatever political party can deny that it is a matter of grave concern to the government.

Even a glance at the situation today only too clearly indicates that equality of opportunity as we have known it no longer exists. Our industrial plant is built. That hardly requires more proof than we see about us constantly. Nevertheless, let us look at our recent history and the simple economics, the kind of economics that you and I and the average man and woman talk.

In the years before 1929 we know that this country had completed a vast cycle of building and inflation; for ten years we expanded on the theory of repairing the wastes of the war, but actually expanded far beyond that, and also far beyond our natural and normal growth. During that time the cold figures of finance prove there was little or no drop in the prices the consumer had to pay, although those same figures prove that the cost of production fell very greatly; corporate profit resulting from this period was enormous; at the same time little of the profit was devoted to the reduction of prices. The consumer was forgotten. Little went into increased wages; the worker was forgotten, and by no means an adequate proportion was paid out in dividends—the stockholder was forgotten.

Incidentally, very little was taken by taxation to the beneficent government of those days.

What was the result? Enormous corporate surpluses piled up—the most stupendous in history. These surpluses went chiefly in two directions: first, into new and unnecessary plants which now stand stark and idle; second, into the call money market of Wall Street, either directly by the corporations or indirectly through the banks.

Then came the crash. Surpluses invested in unnecessary plants became idle. Men lost their jobs; purchasing power dried up; banks became frightened and started calling loans. Those who had money were afraid to part with it. Credit contracted. Industry stopped. Commerce declined, and unemployment mounted.

Translate that within your own knowledge into human terms. See how the events of the past three years have come home to specific groups of people. First, the group dependent upon industry; second, the group dependent upon agriculture; third, that group made up in large part of members of the first two—the "small investors and depositors." Remember that the strongest possible tie between the first two groups, agriculture and industry, is the fact that the savings and to a degree the security of both are tied together in that third group—the credit structure of the nation. We know what has happened to that.

But go back again to the main fact before us today—

that equality of opportunity, as we have known it, no longer exists. Pick up the next tragically obvious economic question—where is opportunity? We must dismiss that historic one which has heretofore been our salvation.

Our last frontier has long since been reached, and there is practically no more free land. More than half our people do not live on farms or on lands and cannot derive a living by cultivating their own property. There is no safety valve in the form of Western prairie to which those thrown out of work by the economic machines can go for a new start. We are not able to invite the immigrants from Europe to share our endless plenty. We are now providing a drab living for our own people.

Our system of constantly rising tariffs has at last reacted against us to the point of closing our Canadian frontier on the north, our European markets on the east, many of our Latin-American markets to the south and a large proportion of our Pacific markets on the west through the retaliatory tariffs of these countries. It has forced many of our great industrial institutions, who exported their surplus production to such countries, to establish plants in those countries, within the tariff walls. This has resulted in the reduction of the operation of their American plants and of opportunity for employment.

Opportunity in business has further narrowed since Wilson's time, just as freedom to farm has ceased. It is still true that men can start small enterprises, trusting to their native shrewdness and ability to keep abreast of competitors; but area after area has been pre-empted altogether by the great corporations, and even in the fields which still have no great concerns the small man starts under a handicap. The unfeeling statistics of the past three decades show that the independent business man is running a losing race. Perhaps he is forced to the wall; perhaps he cannot command credit; perhaps he is "squeezed out," in Wilson's words, by highly organized corporate competitors, as your corner grocery man can tell you.

Recently a careful study was made of the concentration of business in the United States. It showed that our economic life was dominated by some six hundred odd corporations who controlled two-thirds of American industry. Ten million small business men divided the other third.

More striking still, it appeared that, if the process of concentration goes on at the same rate, at the end of another century we shall have all American industry controlled by a dozen corporations and run by perhaps a hundred men. Put plainly, we are steering a steady course toward economic oligarchy, if we are not there already.

Clearly all this calls for a reappraisal of values. A mere builder of more industrial plants, a creator of more railroad systems, an organizer of more corporations, is as likely to be a danger as a help. The day of the great promoter or the financial titan, to whom we granted everything if only he would build or develop, is over.

Our task now is not discovery or exploitation of natural resources or necessarily of producing more goods. It is the soberer, less dramatic business of administering resources and plants already in hand, of seeking to reestablish foreign markets for our surplus production, of meeting the problem of under-consumption, or adjusting production to consumption, of distributing wealth and products more equitably, of adapting existing economic organization to the service of the people.

Just as in older times the central government was first a haven of refuge and then a threat, so now, in a closer economic system the central and ambitious financial unit is no longer a servant of national desire but a danger. I would draw the parallel one step further. We do not think, because national government became a threat in the eighteenth century, that therefore we should abandon the principle of national government.

Nor today should we abandon the principle of strong economic units called corporations merely because their power is susceptible to easy abuse. In other times we dealt with the problem of an unduly ambitious central government by modifying it gradually into a constitutional democratic government. So today we are modifying and controlling our economic units.

As I see it, the task of government in its relation to business is to assist the development of an economic declaration of rights, an economic constitutional order. This is the common task of statesmen and business men. It is the minimum requirement of a more permanently safe order of society. Happily, the times indicates that to create such an order is not only the proper policy of government but is the only line of safety for our economic structure as well.

We know now that these economic units cannot exist

unless prosperity is uniform—that is, unless purchasing power is well distributed throughout every group in the nation. That is why even the most selfish of corporations, for its own interest, would be glad to see wages restored and unemployment aided, and to bring the farmer back to his accustomed level of prosperity, and to assure a permanent safety for both groups. That is why some enlightened industries endeavor to limit the freedom of action of each man and business group within the industry in the common interest of all. That is why business men everywhere are asking for a form of organization which will bring the scheme of things into balance, even though it may in some measure qualify the freedom of action of individual units within the business.

I think that everyone who has actually entered the economic struggle—which means everyone who was not born to safe wealth—knows in his own experience and his own life that we now have to apply the earlier concepts of American government to the conditions of today. The Declaration of Independence discusses the problem of government in terms of a contract. Government is a relation of give and take—a contract, perforce, if we would follow the thinking out of which it grew. Under such a contract rulers were accorded power, and the people consented to that power on consideration that they be accorded certain rights. The task of statesmanship has always been the redefinition of these rights in terms of a changing and growing social order. New conditions impose new requirements upon government and those who conduct government.

The terms of the contract are as old as the Republic and as new as the new economic order. Every man has a right to life, and this means that he has also a right to make a comfortable living. He may by sloth or crime decline to exercise that right, but it must not be denied him. Our government formal and informal, political and economic, owes to every man an avenue to possess himself of sufficient for his needs through his own work. Every man has a right to his own property, which means a right to be assured to the fullest extent attainable, in the safety of his earnings. By no other means can men carry the burdens of those parts of life which in the nature of things afford no chance of labor—childhood, sickness, old age. In all thought of property, this right is paramount; all other property rights must yield to it. If, in accordance with this principle, we must restrict the operations of the speculator, the manipulator, even the financier, I believe we must accept the restriction as needful, not to hamper individualism but to protect it.

The final term of the high contract was for liberty and the pursuit of happiness. We have learned a great deal of both in the past century. We know that individual liberty and individual happiness mean nothing unless both are ordered in the sense that one man's meat is not another man's poison. We know that the old "rights of personal competency"— the right to read, to think, to speak, to choose and live a mode of life—must be respected at all hazards. We know that liberty to do anything which deprives others of those elemental rights is outside the protection of any compact, and that government in this regard is the maintenance of the balance of justice for all.

We shall fulfill our present day governmental obligations, as we fulfilled the obligations of the apparent Utopia which Jefferson imagined for us in 1776 and which Jefferson, Theodore Roosevelt and Wilson sought to bring to realization. We must do so lest a rising tide of misery, engendered by our common failure, engulf us all.

II

NEED FOR ECONOMIC PLANNING

THE EVIDENCES OF change in our social order are so numerous, so tragic in some of their consequences, and so surely indicative of the necessity of sanity in all our planning for the future that there can be no argument with regard to the patriotic and self-sacrificing attitude all men should take who have been given the duty of governing, of legislating and of administering the business of the people.

Our present condition can be expressed, in every industry and profession, by statistics, by charts, by graphic reports. Our hopes for the future may be shown in the same way. While these methods are necessary, I prefer in this discussion to express our problems in planning from the more human and essentially as accurate a point of view.

This view is perhaps sharpest in the eyes of the men and women who are as keenly interested in happiness as any who are at the full tide of their ambition, their health and their youth. I refer to those who have just finished their appointed courses of study and who are ready to prove the value of the most elaborate system of education, not forgetting the cultivation of character, that perhaps the world has ever seen.

In speaking of them I think I best express the youthful attitude which all of us concerned with national planning must maintain if our plans are to be of any use to ourselves as well as to the generations to follow.

Four years ago if they had heard and believed in the tidings of the times, they could expect to take their place in a society well supplied with material things and could look forward to the not too distant time when they would be living in their own homes, each (if they believed the politicians) with a two-car garage, and without great effort would be providing themselves and their families with all the necessities and amenities of life, and perhaps in addition, assure by their savings their security in the future.

Indeed, if they were observant, they would have seen that many of their elders had discovered a still easier road to material success—had found that once they had accumulated a few dollars they needed only to put them in the proper place and then sit back and read in comfort the hieroglyphics called stock quotations which proclaimed that their wealth was mounting miraculously without any work or effort on their part. Many who were called and who are still pleased to call themselves the leaders of finance celebrated and assured us of an eternal future for this easy-chair mode of living. And to the stimulation of belief in this dazzling chimera were lent not only the voices of some of our public men in high office but their influence and the material aid of the very instruments of government which they controlled.

How sadly different is the picture which we see around us today. If only the mirage had vanished, we should not complain, for we should all be better off. But with it have vanished, not only the easy gains of speculation, but much of the savings of thrifty and prudent men and women, put by for their old age and for the education of their children. With these savings has gone, among millions of our fellow citizens, that sense of security to which they have rightfully felt they were entitled in a land abundantly endowed with natural resources and with productive facilities to convert them into the necessities of life for all our population. More calamitous still, there has vanished with the expectancy of future security, the certainty of today's bread, clothing and shelter.

Most of the youth of this country, fit and ready for the work of the world, are either unable to fit into a productive society or gravely concerned over the future, if any, in that place where they have been fortunate enough to find any gainful occupation.

Of course they are hopeful. Much has been written about the hope of youth, but I prefer to emphasize another quality. I hope that a great many have been trained to pursue truths relentlessly and to look at them courageously. I hope that they will face the unfortunate state of the world about them with a greater clarity of vision than many of their elders.

As they have viewed this world of which they are about

to become a more active part, I have no doubt that they have been impressed by its chaos, its lack of plan. This failure to measure true values and to look ahead is true of almost every industry, every profession, every walk of life. Take, for example, the vocation of higher education itself.

If they had been intending to enter the profession of teaching, they should have found that the universities, the colleges, the normal schools of our country were turning out annually far more trained teachers than the schools of the country could possibly use or absorb. The number of teachers needed in the nation is a relatively stable figure, little affected by the depression and capable of fairly accurate estimate in advance with due consideration for our increase in population. And yet, we have continued to add teaching courses, to accept every young man or woman in those courses without any thought or regard for the law of supply and demand. In the State of New York alone, for example, there are at least seven thousand qualified teachers who are out of work—unable to earn a livelihood in their chosen profession, because nobody had the wit or the forethought to tell them in their younger days that the profession of teaching was gravely over-supplied.

Take, again, the profession of the law. Our common sense tells us that we have too many lawyers and that thousands of them, thoroughly trained, are either eking out a bare existence or being compelled to work with their hands, or are turning to some other business in order to keep themselves from becoming objects of charity. The universities, the bar, the courts themselves have done little to bring this situation to the knowledge of young men who are considering entering any one of the multitude of law schools. Here again, foresight and planning have been notable for their complete absence.

In the same way we cannot review carefully the history of our industrial advance without being struck by its haphazardness, with the gigantic waste with which it has been accomplished—with the superfluous duplication of productive facilities, the continual scrapping of still useful equipment, the tremendous mortality in industrial and commercial undertakings, the thousands of dead-end trails in which enterprise has been lured, the profligate waste of natural resources.

Much of this waste is the inevitable by-product of progress in a society which values individual endeavor and which is susceptible to the changing tastes and customs of the people of which it is composed. But much of it, I believe, could have been prevented by greater foresight, and by a larger measure of social planning.

Such controlling and directive forces as have been developed in recent years reside to a dangerous degree in groups having special interests in our economic order, interests which do not coincide with the interests of the nation as a whole. I believe that the recent course of our history has demonstrated that, while we may utilize their expert knowledge of certain problems and the special facilities with which they are familiar, we cannot allow our economic life to be controlled by that small group of men whose chief outlook upon the social welfare is tinctured by the fact that they can make huge profits from the lending of money and the marketing of securities—an outlook which deserves the adjectives "selfish" and "opportunist."

There is a tragic irony in our economic situation today. We have not been brought to our present state by any natural calamity—by drouth or floods or earthquakes, or by the destruction of our productive machine or our man power. We have a superabundance of raw materials, of equipment for manufacturing these materials into the goods which we need, and transportation and commercial facilities for making them available to all who need them. A great portion of our machinery and our facilities stand idle, while millions of able-bodied and intelligent men and women, in dire need, are clamoring for the opportunity to work. Our power to operate the economic machine which we have created is challenged.

We are presented with a multitude of views as to how we may again set into motion that economic machine. Some hold to the theory that the periodic slowing down of the machine is one of its inherent peculiarities, a peculiarity which we must grin about and bear, because if we attempt to tamper with it we shall cause even worse trouble. According to this theory, as I see it, if we grin and bear long enough, the economic machine will eventually begin to pick up speed and in the course of an indefinite number of years will again attain the maximum number of revolutions signifying what we have been wont to miscall prosperity— but which, alas, is but a last ostentatious twirl of the economic machine before it again succumbs to that mysterious impulse to slow down again.

This attitude toward our economic machine requires not only greater stoicism but greater faith in immutable economic law and less faith in the ability of man to control what he has created than I, for one, have. Whatever elements of truth lie in it, it is an invitation to sit back and do nothing; and all of us are suffering today, I believe, because this comfortable theory was too thoroughly implanted in the minds of some of our leaders, both in finance and in public affairs.

Other students of economics trace our present difficulties to the ravages of the World War and its bequest of unsolved political and economic and financial problems. Still others trace our difficulties to defects in the world's monetary systems.

Whether it be an original cause, an accentuating cause, or an effect, the drastic change in the value of our monetary unit in terms of the commodities it will buy is a problem which we must meet straightforwardly. It is self-evident that we must either restore commodities to a level approximating their dollar value of several years ago or else that we must continue the destructive process of reducing, through defaults or through deliberate writing down, obligations assumed at a higher price level.

Possibly because of the urgency and complexity of this problem some of our economic thinkers have been occupied with it to the exclusion of other phases of as great importance.

Of these other phases, that one which seems most important to me in the long run is the problem of controlling, by adequate planning, the creation and the distribution of those products which our vast economic machine is capable of yielding.

I do not mean to curtail the use of capital. I do not mean to curtail new enterprise. But think carefully of the vast sums of capital or credit which in the past decade have been devoted to unjust enterprises—to the development of unessentials and to the multiplication of many products far beyond the capacity of the nation to absorb. It has been the same story as the thoughtless turning out of too many school teachers and too many lawyers.

In the field of industry and business many of those whose primary solicitude is confined to the welfare of what they call capital have failed to read the lessons of the past few years and have been moved less by calm analysis of the needs of the nation as a whole than by a blind determination to preserve their own special stakes in the economic order.

I do not mean to intimate that we have come to the end of the period of expansion. We shall continue to need capital for the production of newly invented devices, for the replacement of equipment worn out or rendered obsolete by our technical progress. A great deal will have to be done to make us decent, healthy, and as happy as our several natures will permit. We need better housing in most of our cities. Many parts of our country still need more and better roads. There is urgent necessity for canals, parks and other physical improvements.

But it seems to me that our physical economic plant will not expand in the future at the same rate at which it has been expanded in the past. We may build more factories, but the fact remains that we have enough to supply all of our domestic needs, and more, if they are used. With these factories we can now make more shoes, more textiles, more steel, more radios, more automobiles, more of almost everything than we can use.

Our basic trouble was not an insufficiency of capital. It was an insufficient distribution of buying power, coupled with an over-sufficient speculation in production. While wages rose in many of our industries, they did not as a whole rise proportionately to the reward to capital, and at the same time the purchasing power of other great groups of our population was permitted to shrink. We accumulated such a superabundance of capital that our great bankers were vying with each other, some of them employing questionable methods, in their efforts to lend this capital at home and abroad.

I believe that we are at the threshold of a fundamental change in our economic thought. I believe that in the future we are going to think less about the producer and more about the consumer. Do what we may to inject health into our ailing economic order, we cannot make it endure for long unless we can bring about a wiser, more equitable distribution of the national income.

It is well within the inventive capacity of man, who has built up this great social and economic machine capable of satisfying the wants of all, to insure that all who are willing and able to work receive from it at least the necessities of life. In such a system, the reward for a day's work will have to be greater, on the average, than it has been, and the reward to capital, especially capital which is speculative, will have to be less.

But I believe that after the experience of the last three years, the average citizen would rather receive a smaller return upon his savings in return for greater security for the principal, than to experience for a moment the thrill or the prospect of being a millionaire only to find the next moment that his fortune, actual or expected, has withered in his hand because the economic machine has again broken down.

It is toward stability that we must move if we are to profit by our recent experience. Few will disagree that the goal is desirable. Yet many of faint heart, fearful of change, sitting tightly to the roof-tops in the flood, will sternly resist striking out for this objective lest they fail to attain it. Even among those who are willing to attempt the journey there will be violent differences of opinion as to how it should be made. So complex, so widely distributed over our whole country are the problems which confront us that men and women of common aim do not agree upon the method of attacking them. Such disagreement leads to doing nothing, to drifting. Agreement may come too late.

Let us not confuse objectives with methods. Too many so-called leaders of the nation fail to see the forest because of the trees. Too many of them fail to recognize the necessity of planning for definite objectives. True leadership calls for the setting forth of the objectives and the rallying of public opinion in support of these objectives.

When the nation becomes substantially united in favor of planning the broad objectives of civilization, then true leadership must unite thought behind definite methods.

The country needs and, unless I mistake its temper, the country demands bold, persistent experimentation. It is common sense to take a method and try it; if it fails, admit it frankly and try another. But above all, try something. The millions who are in want will not stand by silently forever while the things to satisfy their needs are within easy reach.

We need enthusiasm, imagination and ability to face facts, even unpleasant ones, bravely. We need to correct by drastic means if necessary the faults in our economic system from which we now suffer. We need the courage of the young.

III

STATE PLANNING FOR
LAND UTILIZATION

I WISH TO cite the example of an economic plan which has been put into effect and which is still in its experimental stages, yet is not only without detriment to any class of citizen or interest but is certainly and positively proving itself more and more valuable to a very considerable mass of the population in this country. Thirteen million men and women are involved in it and I feel sure great many millions more will be in the future. I refer to the state planning of the use of land for industry and agriculture in the State of New York, a plan which I confidently feel will prove practicable to the nation as a whole.

The problem arises out of the dislocation of a proper balance between urban and rural life. A phrase that covers all its aspects is "Land Utilization and State Planning."

Land utilization involves more than a mere determining of what each and every acre of land can be used for, or what crops it can best grow. That is the first step; but having made that determination, we arrive at once at the larger problem of getting men, women and children—in other words, population—to go along with a program and carry it out.

It is not enough to pass resolutions that land must, or should, be used for some specific purpose. Government itself must take steps with the approval of the governed to see that plans become realities.

This, it is true, involves such mighty factors as the supply and not the over-supply of agricultural products; it involves making farm life far more attractive both socially and economically than it is today; it involves the possibilities of creating a new classification of our population.

We know from figures of a century ago that seventy-five percent of the population lived on farms and twenty-five percent in cities. Today the figures are exactly reversed. A generation ago there was much talk of a back-to-the-farm movement. It is my thought that this slogan is outworn. Hitherto, we have spoken of two types of living and only two—urban and rural. I believe we can look forward to three rather than two types in the future, for there is a definite place for an intermediate type between the urban and the rural, namely, a rural-industrial group.

I can best illustrate the beginnings of the working out of the problem by reviewing briefly what has been begun in the State of New York during the past three years toward planning for a better use of our agricultural, industrial and human resources.

The State of New York has definitely undertaken this as a governmental responsibility. Realizing that the maladjustment of the relationship between rural and city life had reached alarming proportions, the State Administration undertook a study of the agricultural situation with the immediate purpose of relieving impossible and unfair economic conditions on the farms of the State. The broader ultimate purpose was to formulate a well thought out and scientific plan for developing a permanent agriculture.

The immediate situation was met by the enactment of several types of laws that resulted in the relief of farms from an uneven tax burden and made a net saving to agriculture of approximately twenty-four million dollars a year.

First, the State developed additional State aid for rural education, especially in the communities which are so sparsely settled that one-room schools predominate. This State aid gave the smaller rural schools the same advantages already enjoyed by the schools in the larger communities.

Second, a fair equalization of State aid to towns for the maintenance of dirt roads was accomplished by putting it on the basis of mileage rather than of assessed valuation.

Third, through a gasoline tax, additional aid was given to the counties for the development of a definite system of farm-to-market roads.

Fourth, the State embarked on a definite program of securing cheaper electricity for the agricultural communities. It proposes to harness the St. Lawrence River as part of this program, and the electricity developed is by the new law intended primarily for the farmer, the household user, and the small industrialist or store-keeper rather than for large industrial plants.

This was the program to relieve immediate needs.

In all this work, it is worth recording that not only the immediate program but also the long-time planning was worked out in a wholly non-partisan manner. It received the benefits of study by the Legislature and legislative commissions. Much of the program was worked out by the Governor's Agricultural Advisory Commission. This Commission consisted of representatives of great farm organizations such as the Grange, the Farm and Home Bureau, Master Farmers, the Dairymen's League, the G.F.L., members of the Legislature, representatives of State Colleges and various departments of the State government. It received the hearty cooperation of the Mayors' Conference, and that of business men who were willing to give thought to the future of the State and the nation.

The program for the future was worked out upon that common sense basis which must be the core of every economic plan that will come up for consideration. Details cannot be brushed aside for they all dovetail into the larger ultimate picture.

We knew that out of the thirty million acres in the State, three million were in cities, villages, residential areas; five million were in mountains and forests, and by the way, of this five million the State itself had about two million acres in the great Catskill and Adirondack preserves; four million acres were once farmed but now abandoned, leaving a total of eighteen million acres for agriculture, divided into one hundred and sixty thousand farms.

The first definite step was to start a survey of the entire State. This involved a study of all the physical factors both above and below the surface of the soil, and a study of economic and social factors. The study was divided into six important sections. The soil was analyzed. The climate was determined—that is, the length of growing season between killing frosts, and the amount of annual rainfall. The present use of the land was surveyed—whether forest, swamp or improved, in pasture, in hay or in annual crops, and what crops. Those who lived on this land were investigated—who owned it and how he used it—that is, whether to make his livelihood out of it or to occupy it only as a house while working away from the farm in the city or elsewhere. A more specific census of those who lived on this land was made; whether they were old people who had always been there, or new people who had recently come; whether Americans or foreigners; whether the young people were staying on the land or leaving it; whether the cultivation of the farm was supporting the farmer in accordance with an American standard of living. Finally, the measure of the contribution that each farm was making to the food supply of the nation was gauged.

It seemed most desirable to make this survey so detailed that it would give separate data for each ten acre square. Already one county has thus been surveyed and we expect to cover the entire eighteen million acres within the next ten years or less.

The survey is being made on the assumption that good economics require the use of good materials. For example, fifty years ago, the State of New York every year mined thousands of tons of iron ore and turned it into iron and steel. The discovery and the development of the vast fields of a more economical grade of iron ore in Minnesota and the other sections of the country forced the closing of the New York State iron mines. The raw materials did not meet the economic standard. By the same token it may have been profitable when land was first cleared to farm this land, but today, with the tremendous competition of good land in this country and in other parts of the world it has become uneconomical to use land which does not produce good crops.

Therefore, we proposed to find out what every part of the State is capable of producing.

From the survey already made we have come to the belief that a certain percentage of the farm land in the State now under cultivation ought to be abandoned for agricultural purposes. It is possible that the percentage will run as high as somewhere between twenty and twenty-five percent.

We are faced with a situation of farmers attempting to farm under conditions where it is impossible to maintain an American standard of living. They are slowly breaking their hearts, their health and their pocketbooks against a stone wall of impossibilities and yet they produce enough farm products to add to the national surplus; furthermore their products are of such low quality that they injure the reputation and usefulness of the better class of farm products of the State which are produced, packed, and shipped along modern economic lines.

If this is true in the State of New York, it is, I am convinced, equally true of practically every other state east of the Mississippi and of at least some of the states west of the Mississippi.

What then are we to do with this sub-marginal land that exists in every state, which ought to be withdrawn from agriculture? Here we have a definite program. First, we are finding out what it can best be used for. At the present time it seems clear that the greater part of it can be put into a different type of crop—one which will take many years to harvest but one which, as the years go by, will, without question, be profitable and at the same time economically necessary—the growing of crops of trees.

This we are starting by a new law providing for the purchase and reforestation of these lands in a manner approved by the State, part of the cost being borne by the county and part by the State. Furthermore, a Constitutional Amendment was voted by the people of the State, providing for appropriations of twenty million dollars over an eleven-year period to make possible the purchase and reforestation of over one million acres of land, which is better suited for forestry than for agriculture.

We visualized also the very definite fact that the use of this sub-marginal agricultural land for forestry will, in the long run, pay for itself (we will get that twenty million dollars back many times over) and will, from the very start, begin to yield dividends in the form of savings from waste.

For instance, the farms to be abandoned will eliminate the necessity of maintaining thousands of miles of dirt roads leading to these farms, the maintenance cost of which averages one hundred dollars a mile a year. The reforestation of these farms will eliminate the need of providing thousands of miles of electric light and telephone lines reaching out into uneconomical territory. The reforestation of these farms will eliminate the upkeep of many small scattered one-room schools which cost approximately fourteen hundred dollars each per year to the State government.

This is why we are confident that over a period of years this State planning will more than pay for itself in a financial saving to the population as a whole.

Modern society moves at such an intense pace that greater recreation periods are necessary, and at the same time our efficiency, state and national, in production is such that more time can be used for recreation. That is increasingly evident this particular year. By reforestation the land can be turned into a great State resource which will yield dividends at once. As one small detail of this plan, the Conservation Commissioner was able to throw open for hunting and fishing the twenty-five thousand acres recently purchased. He will do the same with additional reforestation areas when they are purchased.

These reforested areas are largely at the higher elevations at the headwaters of streams. Reforestation will regulate stream flow, aid in preventing floods and provide a more even supply of pure water for villages and cities.

What will be done for the population now residing on these sub-marginal lands? First, most of the comparatively small number of people on these farms which are to be abandoned will be absorbed into the better farming areas of the State. Second, we are continuing the idea of the State-wide plan by studying the whole future population trend; here is where there is a definite connection between the rural dweller and the population engaged in industry, between the rural dweller and the city dweller, between the farmer and the people engaged in industry.

Experiments have already been made in some states looking to a closer relationship between industry and agriculture. These take two forms—first, what may be called the bringing of rural life to industry; second, the bringing of industry to agriculture by the establishment of small industrial plants in areas which are now wholly given over to farming.

In this particular connection the State of Vermont, through a splendid commission, seems to be taking the lead in seeking to bring industry to the agricultural regions.

For example, in a valley in Vermont a wood-turning factory for the making of knobs for the lids of kettles has already been so successful that the trend of the rural population to the city has been definitely stopped and the population of the valley finds that it can profitably engage in agriculture during the summer with a definite wage-earning capacity in the local factory during the winter months.

Another example is that of one of the larger shoe manufacturers established in a New York village. Many of the workers live in this village and many others live in the open country within a radius of ten miles or more.

As a nation we have only begun to scratch the surface along these lines and the possibility of diversifying our industrial life by sending a fair proportion of it into the rural districts. Cheap electric power, good roads and automobiles make such a rural-industrial development possible. Without question there are many industries which can succeed just as well, if not better, by bringing them to rural communities. At the same time these communities will be given higher annual income capacity. We will be restoring the balance.

Through such state planning as I have just outlined many of the problems of transportation, of over-crowded cities, of high cost of living, of better health for the race, of a better balance for the population as a whole, can be solved by the states themselves during the coming generation.

These experiments should and will be worked out in accordance with conditions which vary greatly in different sections of the country. I have said "by the states themselves" because some of the state methods of approaching the problem may not be economically sound in the light of future experiences, whereas others may point the way toward a definite national solution of the problems.

I remember that many years ago when James Bryce was Ambassador from England in Washington he said: "The American form of government will go on and live long after most of the other forms of government have fallen or been changed, and the reason is this: In other nations of the world when a new problem comes up it must be tested in a national laboratory, and a solution of the problem must be worked out, and when it is worked out that solution must be applied to the nation as a whole. Sometimes it may be the correct solution and other times it may be the wrong solution. But you in the United States have forty-eight laboratories and when new problems arise you can work out forty-eight different solutions to meet the problem. Out of these forty-eight experimental laboratories, some of the solutions may not prove sound or acceptable, but out of this experimentation history shows you have found at least some remedies which can be made so successful that they will become national in their application."

In state economic planning the state needs the sympathetic cooperation of the national government, if as only an information-gathering body. The national government can and should act as a clearing-house for all of the Governors to work through. I am very confident that during the next few years state after state will realize, as has New York, that it is a definite responsibility of government to reach out for new solutions for the new problems. In the long run state and national planning is an essential to the future prosperity, happiness and the very existence of the American people.

IV

REORGANIZATION OF GOVERNMENT

THE URGENT NECESSITY for economic planning by those at the head of affairs makes essential the clearest possible thinking. When lines of action are established the whole-hearted cooperation is required of all concerned—and this means the support and the action of the intelligent and locally controlling groups of our citizens.

Simple honesty in the carrying out of plans is not enough; a greater efficiency than we have heretofore seen is urgent. As far as the government is concerned with economic plans, their success can be imperiled if we do not put our governmental organization in order for this duty.

My efforts to bring about the reorganization and the consolidation of departments of the national administration, for economy and efficiency in this duty, will constitute a chapter to be written in action. I hope thus to reduce the cost of the regular operations of the Federal Government by no less than twenty-five percent.

But the Federal Government with its very great responsibilities to the individual citizen is not, however, all of the government in this country. I will not attempt to define here the Federal and States' rights and responsibilities. It is sufficient to say that the local government is the point of contact with the average citizen, and whatever the Federal Government may or may not do to intelligently assist his life and his future, the action of his local government is what most closely and most quickly affects him.

Local government is the instrument by which every essential action in the next few years will succeed or fail. Indifference to it is stupid, if it is not criminally negligent. Let us examine local government in this country.

The cost of government in this country, particularly that of local government, is causing considerable concern. The aggregate expenditure of federal, state and local government is approximately twelve or thirteen billion dollars annually. Of this sum the Federal Government spends approximately one-third, state governments about thirteen percent, leaving considerably more than one-half as the cost of local government.

Notwithstanding the influence of the World War on Federal governmental expenditures, the ratios have existed with slight variations since 1890. It is manifest that inasmuch as the cost of local government constitutes the major portion of our aggregate tax bill, we must, if we hope for lower taxes or less rapid increase in taxes, analyze local government and see if its workings may not be simplified and made less expensive for the taxpayer.

The form of local, county and town government, as we know it in most of our states, dates back to the Duke of

York's Laws, enacted about 1670. The design was to meet conditions as they existed at that time. They were continued by the American states after the Revolutionary War. It is astonishing how few changes have been made in their form since the formation of the nation. We may assume that at the time of their adoption they were suited for the conditions of the period.

There were no steamboats, railroads, telephones, telegraphs, motor vehicles or good roads in existence. Means of transportation and communication were meager. The swiftest means of travel and of communication were the saddle horse, the stage coach and the canal. Sometimes we hear the past referred to as the "horse and buggy age." Perhaps it would be more accurate to describe the time of the organization of our local governments as the "ox-cart age." We had no urban centers—only a few overgrown villages. Our population was almost exclusively rural. In those days at least eight out of ten workers obtained a living by tilling the soil. The people lived in small territorial groups and led local community lives. They subsisted almost entirely on the things which they produced or which were produced by others in their own locality. A town form of government was the natural form. It suited the conditions of the times.

Moreover, the need for governmental service was not extensive. Trails met the need of the limited intercommunity travel where expensive motor routes are now necessary. There might be a village pump, but otherwise each citizen took care of his own water supply, and drainage and garbage disposal were family concerns. At first, police and fire protection were not considered municipal functions. Every community made provisions for its own poor. An education in the three R's was deemed sufficient for the average child.

It is not necessary to draw the comparison between those times and today, but there is a particular instability apparent today which renders the old forms of local government more obsolete than they self-evidently are. This is the fact that our population has become, in greater and greater part, transient. We follow the call of industry, of ambition and of whim from community to community and from state to state. It is not only in the newer regions of America that the old resident may find himself in the minority. The personnel and even the character of the population in any village in any one of our older states may change within a few years of rapidly shifting groups whose members are units in a national economic and social scheme rather than fixed residents of any community.

Matters which were originally of local or community concern are now of much wider interest. This applies to such things as roads, schools, public health, the care of the socially dependent and virtually every activity of local government. Yet we have continued to use the machine, designed under radically different conditions, as the major instrument through which to sell governmental service in this age of bewildering movement.

As the machinery of local government exists today, we have, very probably, five hundred thousand units of government. They range from the Federal Government down to the smallest school or special district. Take my own State of New York as an instance. We have sixty-two counties and sixty cities. But this is a mere beginning; we have nine hundred and thirty-two towns and, according to the last count, five hundred and twenty-five villages, nine thousand six hundred school districts and two thousand three hundred and sixty-five fire, water, lighting, sewer and sidewalk districts, a grand total of thirteen thousand five hundred and forty-four separate, independent, governmental units.

Carrying the analysis a step further: In a small densely populated suburban county adjacent to New York City we have three towns and two cities. Again, that is only a start in the complexity of local government; in this same small area we have forty villages, forty-four school districts and one hundred and fifty-six special districts. In this one small county there is a total of two hundred and forty-six governmental units.

We need a simple, smooth running and efficient governmental organization for it to achieve our first necessity—economy of operation.

But with our present complexity the expenditures of local government have increased at an astonishing rate. In 1890 local government in the entire nation cost $487,000,000. In 1927, the last year for which complete figures are available, the government of lesser units within states cost $6,454,000,000. It increased from a per capita of $7.73 in 1890 to $54.41 in 1927.

In the small suburban unit to which I referred, all local taxes in 1900 amounted to $337,000 and in 1929, in round figures, $22,000,000. In that space of time the valuation of taxable property increased thirty-five times, but the taxes increased sixty-five times, while population multiplied only five and one-half times. In another case, that of a rural, agricultural county, local taxes amounted to $158,000 in 1900 and to $1,150,000 in 1929. In this case taxes were multiplied seven times, tax valuations slightly more than two times, while the population of the county actually decreased five percent. In the suburban county per capita local taxes in 1900 were $6 and in the rural county $4.30, but in 1929 they were $90 and $52.

Later I shall discuss taxation and the financing of governmental units. Here, I wish to stress the matter of the organization of these units. Though various measures have gone far toward equalizing the tax load throughout New York State, the fact remains that we are still supporting a complicated machine of local government which seems to me to be unreasonable, expensive, wasteful and inefficient. In our efforts so far we have succeeded in reducing somewhat in the aggregate the cost of this elaborate machine. This same condition exists in every state of the Union. I use the State of New York as an example merely because as Governor of that State for two terms I am intimately familiar with the details of the problem there.

If we look the facts in the face we see an amazing situation. No citizen of the State of New York can live under less than four governments—federal, state, county and city. If he lives in a town outside of a village, he is under five layers of government—federal, state, county, town and school. If he lives in an incorporated village, another layer is added. If he lives in a town outside of a village, he may be in a fire, water, sewer, lighting and sidewalk district, in which case there are ten layers of government.

A citizen so situated has too much governmental machinery to watch. It is too complicated for him to understand. He may not realize that ten sets of officials are appropriating public funds, levying taxes and issuing bonds. His attention is not usually centered on local government, for seldom, if ever, does he know what sums are being appropriated, what taxes are being levied or what bonds issued. Means for gaining information concerning these things are altogether inadequate. Even the editors of the local newspapers do not know what is the governmental action about them, unless there is some particular case which draws attention to details.

There is no real need for so many overlapping units of government.

There is excuse but no necessity for the vast army of useless officials we are carrying upon our backs. Let me give a few simple facts.

In county and town governments alone in New York State, leaving out incorporated cities and villages altogether, there are about fifteen thousand officials, most of whom are elective and have constitutional status. These include in the counties chiefly county judges, sheriffs, surrogates, county clerks, registrars, district attorneys, coroners, county attorneys, and commissioners of welfare; and in the towns, supervisors, town clerks, justices of the peace, assessors, town collectors, highway superintendents, constables, and welfare officers. These paid officers, with minor exceptions, are found in all counties and towns. They constitute what may be called the regular Army of Occupation. But besides this army of occupation there is an even greater corps of what I would call the Home Guards, paid and unpaid, part and whole time, elective and appointive, representing the police, light, fire, sewer, sidewalk, water, and other local improvement districts and the school districts with their boards, superintendents, clerks, and teachers.

To illustrate, take just one case. Leaving out of the picture the five counties within the City of New York, and the wholly suburban counties of Westchester and Nassau, and looking at the other fifty-five counties of the State, there are in the neighborhood of eleven thousand tax collectors! These eleven thousand tax collectors represent nine hundred and eleven towns, four hundred and sixty-one villages and over nine thousand school districts—an average density of tax collectors alone of about twelve per town. It is interesting to note that these eleven thousand tax collectors form a greater army than that which won the battle of Marathon. Note, too, that this huge force is actually responsible for the collection of only about one-sixth of the property tax levied for all purposes within the State. The remaining five-sixths is collected by less than two hundred city, county, town and village officers.

The great majority of the county and town officials I have mentioned are salaried officers, but fees of unknown amount are still allowed to many of them. We have been trying to get away from the ancient fee system, but it still remains firmly entrenched in town and county government. This fee system should be abolished without any question, but this is contingent to a considerable degree on the consolidation of local government units and a readjustment of their relations to the county and to the State.

Let me at this point make it clear that this distressful and wasteful condition affecting local government is not that of New York alone. All over the country the mounting burden of taxation is compelling public officials and citizens to direct their attention to reconstruction.

In Pennsylvania, New Jersey, Minnesota, California, Missouri, Michigan, and many other states, corrective measures are now under way. In North Carolina the State has taken over maintenance and repair of all roads including what we would call town roads. In Virginia, while county lines remain, many county functions have been consolidated into districts comprising several counties. In Minnesota a forest area county sparsely settled has been allowed, after a referendum, to abolish township government. In California a commission has recommended radical changes in the State Constitution to set up the county as the responsible agency for the administration of local government. Let me sum up the situation by saying that the movement to improve local government is active everywhere and spreading all over the United States.

The conclusion reached in all the surveys made is that a radical reorganization of local government is needed. It is generally understood that county government is obsolete and that the county as a unit of administration may well be eliminated. It is conceded that it will take time to secure majority support for that proposal, and in the meantime it is urged that counties be consolidated and that a greatly simplified form of county government be set up to replace present cumbersome forms and many officials.

The excessive cost of local government can most effectively be reduced by simplifying the local governmental organization and structure and reallocating the responsibility for performing various services, according to a logical analysis rather than by accident or by tradition. We must consider each service and decide what administrative unit and what size unit can most effectively and economically perform that service. The smaller units of rural government are so unequal in wealth that some are unable to maintain satisfactory roads and schools even with excessively high tax rates, while others with low rates are able to spend generously and even extravagantly.

All overlapping of local jurisdictions should be abolished. One or two layers of local government subordinate to the sovereignty of the state is adequate and we ought seriously to undertake the radical reorganization and reallocation of functions necessary to accomplish the elimination of others.

There is an immediate remedy for the excessive cost of local governments. It is not as effective as reorganization, but it is a step in the right direction that should be taken without delay if local government is to be as effective as it must be in the near future. This is the controlling of local expenditures by state or district authority. It is familiarly referred to as the "Indiana plan."

In that State ten or more taxpayers in a tax district may appeal, to the state tax commission, from the local budget or from a proposed bond issue. After a hearing, the state tax commission may reduce the proposed appropriation or the amount for which bonds may be issued, or eliminate the item altogether.

This is a clear-cut and effective method of controlling local expenditures. It has passed beyond the experimental stage, and the information before me indicates that it is supported by public sentiment. Colorado and New Mexico have modified forms of the Indiana plan. Ohio, Oklahoma and Oregon have adopted the idea, but the control is exercised through district boards. This general method of controlling the cost of local government is worthy of the immediate consideration by the authorities of every state.

The reorganization of local government has been much too long delayed and this fact has cost many an unnecessary dollar and at the same time deprived the people of improvements and services in the way of the better protection of life and property and of better facilities for orderly, happy living that might have been purchased with the same—or less—expenditure.

We all of us recognize, I think, that much of the increase in the aggregate of governmental expense has been inevitable and necessary. The limited summary I have given here in the matter of organization has been sufficient to show that government has been quite properly called upon to assume responsibilities that once belonged to the individual and to the family. In the same way the larger units of government have been properly and logically forced to assume functions that once belonged to the lesser units. The demands of a different sort of civilization and a different sort of national economy have forced us to redistribute the burdens which the public service imposes.

Roads, for instance, are no longer merely local facilities. We face the question of education and find a mandate from the state as sovereign that the children of all shall be given opportunities to learn. We are beginning to recognize that public health is more than a local responsibility. Crime ceased to be a local matter when the criminal adopted a state-wide and a national range.

As to all these matters, I expect and hope soon to see an increased measure of assumption of functions and responsibilities by the state, through one means or another.

An effort to equalize the tax burden usually makes the state holder of the purse strings for a large proportion of the local expenditures. This creates a responsibility for wise expenditure that can hardly be avoided by the state, in justice to those who have been taxed on a state-wide basis to replenish the state's treasury. This responsibility, it seems to me, is fairly certain to result in much closer and more authoritative supervision of all local expenditures. This inevitably means a closer integration of local authority with some competent state authority, based on the fact that, as to many functions, some competent authority, with expert staffs, and state-wide information, will possess both an advisory and a veto power over the use of funds for local expenditure.

It also seems logical that local authority must consolidate, eliminating many of the local governmental layers, in order to retain any appropriate measure of home rule over local affairs.

Too many of us have been lazy-minded in this matter of government. We like to talk in large terms about the comparative advantages and disadvantages of democracy and autocracy; we like patriotically to admire the work of our forefathers in devising our forms of government or to criticize them as too slavish imitators, but we are dilatory in following our forefathers' example by seeking to plan and devise for our own immediate needs and for the future. Particularly, we hate the details of government. We talk about Russia's five-year and ten-year plans and the excellence or iniquity of Mussolini's system, in preference to giving consideration of the question whether a town supervision is good for anything or inquiring what a village health officer does to earn his pay. This may be because it is easier to form a judgment on matters that are more remote. I hate to think that it is because we prefer to have somebody else form our judgments for us.

This suggests to me that those who hold public office should not be content merely to take the duties of their jobs as they find them and to carry them out according to precedent. Those who have had experience in operating the machine should be able to tell of its defects. I once heard of a public official who recommended that his job be abolished as useless. It would be a heartening and refreshing thing if there were a lot more like him.

.We heard a great deal during the Great War about the challenge to democracy and I think it was a good thing for our complacency to learn that democracy was being challenged. But democracy is being challenged today just as forcibly if not as clamorously. The challenge is from all who complain about the inefficiency, the stupidity and the expense of government. It may be read in the statistics of crime and in the ugliness of many of our communities. It is expressed in all the newspaper accounts of official graft and blundering. It is written in our tax rules and even in the patriotic-seeming text books that our children study in the schools. It looms large on election day when voters see before them long lists of names of men and women of whom they have never heard to be voted upon as candidates for salaried offices of whose duties and functions the voter has but the haziest impression.

The men who addressed themselves to the task of laying the framework of our national government after freedom had been won, wrote down in enduring words that their aim was to form "a more perfect union." In writing that ideal into the preamble of the Constitution of the United States, I think they set a task for us as well as for themselves.

They were forming a new government suited, as they believed, to the conditions of their day, but they were wise enough to look into the future and to recognize that the conditions of life and the demands upon government were bound to change as they had been changing through ages past, and so the plan of government that they had prepared was made, not rigid but flexible—adapted to change and progress.

We cannot call ourselves either wise or patriotic if we seek to escape the responsibility of remolding government to make it more serviceable to all the people and more responsive to modern needs.

V

Expenditure and Taxation

IT IS OBVIOUS that the problem of taxation is one of the greatest before us. Here, again, it is possible to reach a solution if the methods of sane economic planning are brought into play. But it must be remembered that if we are going to do anything about the reduction of taxes and about the readjustment of their burden, at the same time we must work out the solution of other governmental problems with which it is meshed and have the courage to apply these solutions. Nearly half our total tax bill is local.

Taxes take us back again into a consideration of the functions of government and any consideration of them must weave a pattern of finance from beginning to end. That is why in most cases it is impossible to isolate a detail of government, whether a detail of actuality or of hope, from its cost.

The modern state is going into business, whether it likes it or not. We are being forced into business by modern civilization. In the old days, for example, we would put up a building, and the unfortunate insane in our midst were placed in that building. They were then and thereafter forgotten by the people of the state.

We did not even cover all the insane in the state. There were thousands of them, scattered about in the various communities, hidden away in back rooms and attics. There were mentally deficient children all over the state, for whom the state did nothing in those days. There were prisons in those days that had been built sixty or seventy years before, with cells in them that were six feet six inches long, thirty inches wide, with seven feet of headroom—and even twenty years ago we thought that was right. We still have these accommodations in use. I am using this as an illustration, because it has only been in the last ten years that there has been a growing feeling on the part of modern civilization that we have not been handling the wards of the state rightly.

In 1930 in the State of New York we had somewhere around sixty or seventy thousand wards of the State. That does not include the wards of the various counties and cities and other communities. Modern civilization has made us revise our whole plan of handling them.

We are now, in the case of the insane, for example, constantly making new improvements in the study of psychiatry. We are curing people who even twenty years ago would have been pronounced incurable. In fact the ratio of improvement has constantly risen, so that in 1930 we were curing somewhere between twenty and twenty-two percent of these unfortunates. To refer again to prisons, we are looking toward the ideal day when of the ninety-four percent of the prisoners who come back again into our hands, the very great majority of them will go straight all the rest of their lives. We already have a better system worked out under which this is more than possible.

Of necessity, the State has gone into things that did not exist twenty years ago as State problems—highways, for instance. At that time we had a plan, a magnificent plan it seemed, to cost ten or fifteen million dollars, to build main highways from New York to Buffalo, from Albany to Montreal, and there was no such reason to go to Montreal as there is today. Today it is not just the main highways that are concrete. The farmer on every back road is asking for concrete past his door.

There is another reason why the expenditures of the states have gone up. The educational standards are higher. In 1920 the State of New York was extending State aid for education at a cost of ten million dollars; it is now extending it at the cost of more than one hundred million. Nearly one-third of all the expenditures of the State government are going as aids to education. Perhaps this is not the right policy, but it seems to be in line with modern thought, and I do not believe there is anybody who can suggest any alternative that would not be reactionary.

There are real reasons for the increase in the cost of government besides the growing inefficiencies in its organization that I have pointed out in a previous chapter.

I do not wish to set up too detailed a picture of the difficulties. But a clear understanding of the problem requires that examples be used to illustrate the trends of state government. These trends are so important that, as Governor of the State of New York, I sought again and again to bring them to the attention of the public. Familiarity with them brings agreement upon the kind of action that will have to be taken to reduce taxation.

Take at random the expenditure conditions within several of the essential departments of the State government, as illustrated in New York.

Look at the Departments of Correction and Social Welfare. Perhaps no two state departments illustrate better than do these the fact that public services are created and enlarged from time to time in response to public opinion. At the same time, they also illustrate that alteration of the essential scheme and services of government can be made only when changing public opinion leads to changes in the laws which control the scope and cost of government.

The Department of Correction operates seven State prisons, two reformatories, two hospitals for the criminal insane, two institutions for defective delinquents and one school for juvenile delinquents. In 1931 this department spent eight and a half million dollars, seventy-eight percent more than ten years previously. The number of inmates of these institutions was about thirteen thousand, fifty percent more than in 1922. The prison population is growing. Here is a department with a cost increase of some three million seven hundred thousand dollars in ten years. The factors of the increase are easy to trace, but let us look at the increase in its broader, more significant outlines.

The central fact is that the number of prisoners has increased. If, in ten years, we made no change in the food,

clothing, housing and treatment of prisoners, our penal institutions in this one state would be costing one million
three hundred and twenty-five thousand dollars more a
year than they did in 1922. This is nearly half of the ten-
year increase. It is the result of the Baumes laws and other
amendments of the criminal code by which sentences were
made more severe, time allowances for good behavior were
reduced, and the granting of paroles was restricted. The
trend is unchangeable as long as present laws covering
the commitment and detention of prisoners are in force.
The other half of the increased cost since 1922 came because we have provided better prison facilities. I need not
detail these; there is good and sufficient reason for them on
the grounds of decency alone. Reducing prison costs is a
question of administration in an only negligible degree. It
is in the largest sense a question of social and public policy.
It comes to the questions: How much imprisonment of men
and women convicted of crime do you wish to buy? How
much are you willing to pay for?

Public opinion has had an even more unmistakable effect on the costs of the Department of Social Welfare. The
appropriation for this department was two hundred and
ninety thousand dollars in 1922. It remained at about that
level for years. But in 1932 it shot up to nine million one
hundred thousand, almost solely on account of old-age security legislation which placed new responsibilities on the
State.

Does the State wish to save more than eight millions of
dollars annually by repealing the provisions for its contri-

bution to old-age pensions, turning the full responsibility for the care of the aged poor back to cities and counties, and returning to the standards of 1922 in this field?

Take the State Department of Labor. The workmen know that it is the agency through which they may be able to get jobs. Even in 1931 it placed more than one hundred thousand in jobs. The merchant or the manufacturer in the State of New York knows that it is the agency which adjusts differences between him and his employees, and tells him specific improvements which he should or must make in order to protect the health and safety of his workers. Agents of this Department in 1931 made more than eight hundred and fifty thousand inspections of the establishments of manufacturers and merchants.

This is the State agency which is striving day in and day out to prevent the exploitation of labor, to enforce child labor laws, to safeguard women in industry, to keep the disabled worker from becoming a charge upon the community, to reduce the risks of further catastrophes such as the Triangle Fire of 1911 in which one hundred and forty-seven lives were lost. This is the intensely human realm which we have to look at from a strictly cost standpoint.

The Department cost three million three hundred thousand dollars to operate in 1931. That was one million seven hundred thousand dollars more than it cost ten years before, or more than twice as much. What caused the increase? Was it wise? Should the policies which caused it be reversed in order that taxes might be lower?

In a large sense, the answer depends upon the point of

view. The nineteenth century philosophers placed little or no store in the idea of government recognizing or discharging broad social obligations. If you share this narrow view, you might regard this Department of Labor as an improper activity of the state, however socially useful its services might be.

On the other hand, perhaps you share the concept of government so ably stated by Sean T. O'Kelly, the Irish Free State's delegate at the Imperial Economic Congress at Ottawa recently. He described the aim of the modern state as being "to provide such economic conditions as will allow the greatest possible number of people to live in peace and comfort." If that is your view, you might easily believe that this Department of Labor, instead of spending too much, may perhaps not be spending enough.

One particular item of eighty thousand dollars is in the overhead, administrative and statistical work of this Department. Whether all of this expenditure is justifiable may be debatable, but it is significant that New York has been almost the only state in the country with sufficient statistical knowledge of unemployment to permit it to build its remedies along practical lines consistent with actual conditions. If major services of the Department were to be cut to earlier levels, overhead costs automatically would tend to return to their former amounts. Should we return to 1922 standards of administrative direction and statistical control of this work in order to save eighty thousand dollars?

Look at the Department of Agriculture and Markets. Ten years ago, we bought from the Department twenty specific services for the people at a cost, in round figures, of one million nine hundred thousand dollars. In 1932 we bought thirty-four separate services at a cost of five million seven hundred thousand. How intimately associated is this department with the lives of the people? Is it necessary or just an expensive luxury? It supervises milk plants; enforces the pure-food laws. It safeguards the food supply of the State, beginning in the process before the seeds of the future food crop are deposited in the ground and continuing until the food is delivered to the door of the consumer. To help the farmer in his work it administers State funds for fairs, disseminates information concerning farm conditions, inspects feed for livestock, examines fertilizers, publishes food production statistics, endeavors to obtain fair rates for the transportation of good products. The Department does not work to suppress bovine tuberculosis because it wants to; it does so because laws have been passed saying that it must.

The cost of the work to eradicate tuberculosis in cattle was by far the largest item. In 1931 it was four million three hundred and ninety-five thousand as compared with seven hundred and ninety-six thousand ten years ago. Do we want to continue to buy this same tuberculosis eradication? Ten years ago the number of accredited herds (those which are freed of infection and certified for the production of milk) was six hundred and eighty-five. At the end of 1931 the number of herds had increased to seventy-five thousand. The work of supervision under the tuberculin test, the slaughtering of infected animals, and the payment of indemnities to owners, all seem essential. The work of eradicating tuberculosis is about two-thirds done.

Since we are upon the subject of health, I will detail a little of the work of the Department of Health and rest the case there. Its cost is not a large part of the total cost of the State government, but it has been increasing rapidly as its services have been extended and as its contacts with the daily life of the people have been enlarged.

There is little possibility of argument over the idea that a healthy people is the most valuable asset a state can have. It transcends in importance all material wealth. But the enlargement of service is a potent influence upon the cost figures. Aside from a three hundred thousand dollar purchase of radium, the State spent for health activities about three million two hundred thousand, more than twice as much as in 1922. Excluding institutional cost, the Department proper cost nine hundred and sixty-five thousand more in 1931 than it did ten years earlier.

Generally, that increase represents developments which have taken place since the time not many years ago when we decided that public health was purchasable. By spending certain sums of money we know that we can purchase for the whole population a larger degree of freedom from particular diseases, such as malaria, yellow fever, typhoid fever and even tuberculosis.

In the work to reduce infant mortality and to promote child hygiene, ten years ago the cost was twenty-three thousand dollars. In 1931 it was seven times greater. During that period there has been a spectacular decline in infant mortality, at least partly attributable to this work. In 1915, of every thousand babies born, one hundred died before they were a year old. On the same basis only seventy died in 1922 and but fifty-nine in 1930. If the 1915 infant death rate had prevailed nine thousand more babies under the age of one year would have died in 1930. Should the State save one hundred and forty-four thousand dollars by restricting the maternity, infancy and child hygiene work to the scope of 1922?

No man in public office today can fail to realize the demand and the need for lower taxes. He knows that business, industry and agriculture are straining under a tax load heavier than they can safely bear. He knows that high taxes are one of the contributive causes of unemployment.

While recognizing these things, the man in public office also knows the facts of government. Taxes grow out of expenditures; expenditures spring from services; services result from the commands of the people, in the form of laws passed by the legislature directing and instructing the administrative branch of the government what to do. If taxes are to be reduced, services must be curtailed or eliminated. That is plain. It is also clear that services can be eliminated or curtailed—not by passionate oratory or by resolutions—but only by new instructions from the people through the legislatures in the form of new laws or the repeal of old laws. Under our plan of government those new instructions are the direct product of public opinion.

That is one side of taxation. The other side is even more amazing. There is practically no basic American principle applying to taxes, which of necessity affects every citizen and every corporation. We find, for instance, that there is no line of demarcation between Federal taxes and state taxes. In many cases there is a definite duplication of taxes by the Federal Government and by the state, as, for example, in the case of the income tax. Also we find that there is duplication and overlapping between state taxes and local taxes with the result that far too often we have subjected ourselves to a double tax on exactly the same property or the same right. Furthermore, we find that the actual burden of taxation is in a very large number of instances unequal.

It seems to me that the time has come for every state to cooperate with every other state in laying down certain lines or programs of taxation which will be sound and at the same time can be understood by the average citizen. The first step is, of course, for the Federal Government to recognize a definite and clear-cut classification of taxes which it wishes reserved to it and for the states to concur. The Federal Government should be limited to this classification, except in time of war or great national emergency. All other methods of taxation would thereby automatically be reserved to the states themselves. This, it seems to me, would carry out the whole spirit and purpose of the Federal Constitution.

With the reserving of all other taxes to the states, the states will then have an opportunity to work out for themselves a second classification of taxes, dividing those taxes into those which the state itself will levy on the one hand, and those which will be reserved for local tax purposes—

counties, cities, school districts and so forth—on the other hand.

When legislators, administrators and voters are able to bring about an orderly dividing of the methods of taxation between the national government, the state governments and the local governmental units—the organization of which as I have pointed out must be sharply simplified—then and only then can we as a nation take up the equally important task of putting some kind of a limit on the total of our taxes and on the total of the government debts which we are so eagerly increasing at the present time.

Not only must government income meet prospective expenditures but this income must be secured on the principle of ability to pay. This is a declaration in favor of graduated income, inheritance and profits taxes, and against taxes on food and clothing, whose burden is actually shifted to the consumers of these necessities of life on a per capita basis rather than on the basis of the relative size of personal incomes.

Something more is needed than a domestic balanced budget and a just revenue system. Muddled government finance creates a general uncertainty concerning the value of national currencies; this uncertainty has a way of spreading from country to country. The United States could well afford to take the lead in asking for a general conference to establish less changeable fiscal relationships and to determine what can be done to restore the purchasing power of that half of the world's inhabitants who are on a silver basis, and to exchange views regarding governmental finance. It is obvious that sound money is an international necessity, not a domestic consideration for one nation alone. Nothing is more needed than such exchanges of opinion; nothing could do more to create a stable condition in which trade could once more be resumed.

If it be considered radical to suggest that government can be made more practical, more efficient and more businesslike, then this is radical doctrine. I am thinking, and all good Americans are thinking, I hope, not just in terms of ourselves and our lifetime. We are thinking, I trust, in terms of the children and the grandchildren who will come after us. It is our sacred obligation to hand over to them cities, villages, counties, states and a nation which will not be a series of millstones about their necks.

VI

SHALL WE REALLY PROGRESS?

OUR GROWING ALARM over the rising cost of government is because the burden of taxation appears to be so rapidly growing in weight that many think it may become intolerable even within our own lifetime. Already this burden is radically affecting our lives. But apart from extravagance, inefficiency and waste we cannot deny that the rising cost is in a considerable measure due to the new concept of government which envisions the greater happiness and security of all the people.

There has been a marked increase of state services available to the average man and woman. These services do not ordinarily come to the attention of those most liable to complain of the very grave social injustices of the times; they demand more service—not being familiar with those already existing. This often brings about duplication.

The real question before us is whether or not we shall allow our economic difficulties and our organization inefficiency to frustrate the wholesome and essential development of our civilization. As I see it, our social aims should spur our attack upon these problems.

Two particular plans for social welfare just coming to the fore vitally affect the whole range of our present and future American civilization. The lives of ninety percent of our citizens—all those who have to work and do not live on investments—are concerned with the possibilities of unemployment (even if they are fortunately now employed) and the possibility of needing outside assistance in their old age. Up to the present the public has not concerned itself greatly with finding a solution, first because as a young nation untouched resources have been open to us, and second, because the social sciences are still in their infancy, and until recently poverty and hunger and want, to a great extent, have been treated as necessary and inevitable evils.

It is necessary briefly to review existing conditions in order to put down in black and white what we seek to remedy. We can and must think nationally, for every state and every region face the same facts and are affected by conditions in every other state and region. A good illustration is an occurrence of 1929. When the automobile industry in Detroit laid off several hundred thousand workers in local plants, forty thousand of these came to the State of New York looking for jobs—a mass movement nearly a third of the way across the continent. Today, because the nation is so greatly industrialized, the closing down of ten percent of industry is felt very definitely in every community.

The absurdity is now obvious of the new economic theory which was foisted upon the nation in 1928 and 1929 that, contrary to all teachings of history, constant work would continue indefinitely on a rising scale just as long as high wages continued, combined with a high pressure selling campaign to dispose of the output. It was all to be bought and paid for if everybody was employed and earning good wages. Thus if every family in the United States owned one automobile and one radio set in 1930, by 1940 every family would need two cars and two radios, by 1950 every family would need three—the older theory of a saturation point having been wholly abandoned. Failure to recognize the old law of supply and demand was criminal enough; but to this was added the spectacle of officials of government and leading financiers juggling with figures in order deliberately to distort facts. When between twelve and fifteen workers out of every hundred are out of a job in very many industries it is neither truthful nor useful to tell them that employment is practically back to normal, no matter what purely psychological reasons may stand in the way of output.

The truth of the matter is that we are in the midst of another turn of the wheel in the economic cycle and that production in most instances has outrun consumption. To this domestic crisis has been added a tremendous falling off in our exports. To go into the reason for this would be out of place here.

Next we must consider the effect of the latest manufacturing and selling processes. The result of so-called efficiency methods is that the top age of employment usefulness is no longer from sixty-five to seventy years of age, but has dropped to from forty-five to fifty years of age. Though the practice is happily not universal, a growing number of large employers have been hiring only young men and women, and in times of reduction the older employees have been the first to go. This means that the old-age problem, which only a few years ago was by common consent set at the seventy-year mark, is today advanced to include thousands of people in their first fifties and sixties. How much of this change is due to the last disastrous years may never be known, but this does not alter the probability that the change will further continue.

To sum up the existing situation, we have a highly complex problem here—one in which unemployment and old-age want are becoming more and more interwoven, where the remedy of one must take cognizance of the other, where government aid must be thought out along scientific economic lines and not be tossed out as charity or as a result of political hysteria.

Judging by the past and by the present, unemployment always will be with us as a nation, varying with the economic cycles. Certain trends and steps are being worked out in various sections and in various industries for the purpose of flattening out, at least partially, the peaks and valleys. For example, the trend is distinctly toward the five-day week. This means the employment of more people, or, at least, the laying off of fewer people, as does also the movement toward shorter hours of work per day.

Then we have the movement toward the better planning of work, the so-called Cincinnati system, which guarantees to the worker a definite period of work, say forty-eight weeks out of the year, for which he or she is hired; with this planning goes the staggering of work, the cooperation between different lines of industry and the acceleration of public and private construction in times of depression.

It is a fine thing that practically every state government has recognized the emergency and taken definite action. For instance, in 1930 the Legislature of the State of New York gave me, as Governor, an appropriation of ninety million dollars for public work, an increase of twenty million dollars over the previous year. So, also, the municipalities and counties of the State increased this total fourfold. These, however, are emergency measures and cannot necessarily be counted on in future periods of unemployment because the debts of local governments have increased to an alarming and perhaps dangerous extent.

More permanent remedies have been undertaken in various parts of the country. For example, in New York, a committee appointed by me, composed of four business men, a labor leader and the State Industrial Commissioner, consulted with larger industrial concerns and established the principle of giving steadier work by careful planning within the industries themselves. All these studies and plans, however, are confronted with a definite lack of statistics and facts; for instance, it was known fairly accurately how many people were employed but very inaccurately how many people were unemployed. Here is an immediate need for governmental and private organizing in order that we may have the whole truth about the unemployment situation. Announcements from the high officials in Washington have been discredited—though it is obvious that the true facts are the people's right.

Furthermore, industrial planning, while excellent in the case of larger employers who in some cases can make their output programs for a year or more in advance during normal times, is not so possible for the smaller employer or for the man who in his business handles only one line of goods.

The conclusions, again, are obvious. Careful planning, shorter hours, more complete facts, public works and a dozen other palliatives will in the future reduce unemployment especially in times of industrial depression, but all of these put together will not eliminate unemployment. There may indeed be periods in our future history when, for economic or political reasons, we may have to go through several years of hardship, one right on top of another. We shall have in these periods new "accidents" of employment, such as we have had in the past; for instance, changes in style such as the replacement of cotton goods by artificial silk; or the depression in the spoken drama with the advent of motion pictures and the talkies. So also we shall have new inventions which will be compared to the advent of the automobile and we may have further losses of foreign markets. Some of these changes are predictable, others are not. Against them some form of insurance seems to be the only answer.

We shall come to unemployment insurance in this country just as certainly as we have come to workmen's compensation for industrial injury, just as certainly as we are today in the midst of insuring against old-age want.

Ninety percent of unemployment is wholly without the fault of the worker. Other nations and governments have undertaken various systems which insure their workers when unemployment comes. Why should we, in the forty-eight states of our Union, fear to undertake the task?

It is, of course, necessary for us to guard against two grave dangers. Insurance against unemployment must not, by any chance or loophole, become a mere dole which encourages idleness and defeats its own purpose. It should be possible in developing a system of unemployment insurance to draw a hard and fast line against any man or woman who declines to accept an offered position, and it should be possible so to alternate employment that no individual will be unable to find a job for more than two or three months at a time. The other danger is that there will be a natural tendency to pay the cost of unemployment insurance out of current revenues of government. It is clear that unemployment insurance must be placed upon an actuarial basis, and that contributions must be made by the workers themselves. Ideally, a carefully worked out system of unemployment insurance should be self-supporting and a close and intelligent study of the facts and of the law of averages can make this wholly possible.

The suggestions made by the Interstate Commission on Unemployment Insurance in its report early in 1931 to the Governors' conference on unemployment called by me deserves action to follow. This commission was composed of representatives of six of the seven Eastern industrial states— New York, Ohio, Pennsylvania, New Jersey, Massachusetts and Connecticut.

The plan they worked out is sound and carefully safe-guarded. It would make provision for the irregularity of industrial operation, give incentives for the regularization of industry and maintain the morale and self-respect of the worker, so essential to the citizens of a democracy. It contains a radical departure from all European plans in that it definitely avoids the commingling of reserve and relief funds, recommending that the payments of each employer constitute his reserves which are not to be turned into a common pool.

The payment by each employer is to be a contribution amounting to two percent of his payroll and to be reduced to one percent when the accumulated reserve per employee shall have exceeded fifty dollars. The maximum benefit is to be ten dollars a week or fifty percent of an employee's wage, whichever is lower, and the maximum period of benefit to be ten weeks of any twelve months. The payment by each employer is to constitute the employment reserve of his firm and not to be added to the common pool. The creation of an Unemployment Administration of three members is suggested, one representing labor, one industry and one the general public.

The suggestion is made that the states take prompt steps to extend their public employment service, since no system of unemployment insurance can accomplish its purpose without a properly organized and efficiently operated system of employment exchanges.

The Unemployment Commission is to encourage cooperative action between firms and industries, since the most effective measures for achieving greater stabilization cannot be accomplished by a single firm.

The report names two reasons for recommending contributions to the fund by employers: first, "the employee should not in our judgment be required to reduce his earnings further by the payment of contributions into reserves"; second, "the employer's financial liability under the plan would operate as a continuous incentive to prevent unemployment as far as practicable."

By the recommendation that the payments by each employer constitute the unemployment reserve of his firm and be not added to the common pool, the report hopes to avoid what "has been widely recognized even by sympathetic critics of European practice as having had unfortunate results." When the pooling system is used, according to the report, "the irregular industries enabled to draw benefits for their unemployed workmen from the common pool may thus be tempted to shift responsibility and the cost of their own unemployment to the more stable and profitable industries. Insofar then as an unemployment is due to careless or indifferent management, or to the failure to take proper precautions for the future, the pooling of reserves may have the effect of perpetuating such uneconomic practice, and may, in consequence, fail to offer the incentives to regularization for which many of the advocates of unemployment insurance had hoped."

I feel that these suggestions are practical, as simple as the nature of such action can be, and should be seriously taken up.

With plans for old-age security already taking form in the State of New York, becoming law and getting into operation, despite the financial difficulties of the times, it seems to me to be sure that we are going to continue to progress along lines of social welfare. It is amazing what a revolution has taken place in men's minds in a comparatively short space of time—for twenty years ago there would have been nothing but public laughter or apprehension at the way some of us are viewing the duties of government.

Today, there is no need for a long argument to prove that old-age security logically and inevitably ties in with the whole problem of the unemployed and that something can actually be done about it. Everyone knows that when old men and women are no longer able to support themselves by working, they come into the ranks of the unemployed just as much as if they were the victims of industrial layoffs. The only difference is that their layoff is permanent rather than temporary.

It is of course inevitable that these problems be worked out in a piecemeal manner. For example, the passage of the old-age security law in the State of New York in 1930 took only one short step toward the larger problem. The new law applies only to men and women seventy years old and over, but it is based on the correct theory that it is in the long run cheaper and better for the beneficiaries to live in their own homes during their declining years than for them to become inmates of institutions.

The New York law has failed to go to the real roots of old-age want. It has set up no machinery for the building up of what in time must become an insurance fund to which the State and the workers, and possibly the employers, will contribute. The cost of the present law is to be borne half by the State and half by the counties of the State. That may be very well as a stop-gap to meet the emergency of those who are today in want, but the law must be made broader in its application, doing away definitely with state and county aid and establishing an insurance system by which the worker will become an actual part as an individual the very first day that he or she starts to become a wage-earner in the community.

These social situations must be met with no haphazard answers. The principles of insurance can be made to meet the basic problems of unemployment and old-age want. This is a sound business proposal. It would be far more radical to suggest that local and state governments should, in the days to come, grant pensions or doles to those who are in need.

It is essential that the various states seek to work out these problems. It is probable that they will attack them in ways which differ in method. Yet this is one of the great advantages of our system of forty-eight separate and distinct sovereignties. Some states will, without doubt, be more successful than others. But we can learn by comparisons and the interchange of ideas. So far there has been very little interchange; there must be an active and intelligent interchange from now on.

VII

What About Agriculture?

SOCIAL WELFARE HAS always been associated with the work to be done with the humanities in the crowded industrial centers. Plans for a restoration of the economic balance have also, in the past, been set, all out of proportion to the facts, in these same surroundings. An industrial civilization, the brilliance of a mechanized progress, has made it difficult to remember that one-third of our population in the United States is dependent upon wheat and cotton, for example, for their livelihood and purchasing power.

We all recognize that there is no single factor that will, by itself, bring immediate prosperity to the agricultural population of all parts of the country. I know this personally for four reasons. I lived on a farm in the State of New York for fifty years; I ran a farm in the State of Georgia for eight years; ever since I have been in public life I have made it a point to travel over the country and in so doing I have maintained a practical interest in the farm problems of the various parts of the country at first hand; finally, as Governor of the State of New York, the farm products of which now rank fifth or sixth among the states, I have in four years devoted myself to building a farm program.

At the risk of repeating some details which have been mentioned in previous chapters I must cite examples to illustrate the building up of this program. Existing tax obligations of local communities were lightened to the extent of twenty-four millions a year. State aid for roads was redistributed on a mileage basis instead of on an assessment basis, so that the rural communities could enjoy exactly the same privileges in the improvement of their dirt roads as that given to the richer suburban communities. The same principles of aid were applied to rural schools. The State assumed the entire cost of constructing and reconstructing the roads on the rural highway system. The State paid all except a small fraction of the grade crossing elimination so that safety might be afforded to the less as well as the more fortunate districts. Appropriations for the safeguarding of rural health were increased. The soil survey was started—as detailed in my comment upon land utilization. In addition, the laws relating to cooperative corporations and traffic in farm produce were revised more in the interest of the farmer. Legislation was enacted to create a new system of rural credit organizations to meet the emergency created by the collapse of rural banks.

While most of these are emergency measures which can be taken within the several states, they should be considered merely as contributive to the success of much broader action which must be taken by the Federal Government.

I see no occasion for discussing in detail the acute distress in which the farmers of America find themselves. They receive prices as low or lower than at any time in the history of the United States. The economic turn means nothing less than the shadow of peasantry over six and a half million farm families. These families represent twenty-two percent of the population of the United States. In 1920 they received fifteen percent of the national income, in 1925 eleven percent, in 1928 about nine percent, and in some of the recent estimates based on figures of the United States Department of Agriculture the farm income has dropped to about seven percent.

Fifty million men, women and children immediately within our borders are directly concerned with the present and the future of agriculture. Another fifty or sixty million people who are engaged in business and industry in our large and small civic communities are at last coming to understand the simple fact that their lives and their futures are also profoundly concerned with the prosperity of agriculture. They realize more and more that there will be no outlet for their products unless their fifty million fellow Americans who are directly concerned with agriculture are given the buying power to buy city products.

Our economic life today is a seamless web. Whatever our vocation, we are forced to recognize that while we have enough factories and enough machines in the United States to supply all our needs, these factories will be closed part of the time and the machines will lie idle if the buying power of fifty million people remains restricted or dead.

If we get back to the root of the difficulty, we will find

that it is the present lack of equality for agriculture. Farming has not had an even break in our economic system. The necessities that our farmers buy cost nine percent more than they did before 1914. The things they sell bring them forty-three percent less than they did then. These figures, as of August 1, 1932, authenticated by the Department of Agriculture, mean that the farm dollar of that date was worth less than half of what it represented before the World War.

This means finding a cure for a condition that compels the farmer to trade in 1932 two wagon loads for the things for which in 1914 he traded one wagon load.

There are two undeniable facts during these past twelve years. First, the three last national administrations failed utterly to understand the farm problem as a national whole, or to plan for its relief; and second, they destroyed the foreign markets for our exportable surplus, beginning with the Fordney-McCumber tariff and ending with the Grundy tariff, thus violating the simple principles of international trade and forcing the retaliation of the other nations of the world.

I cannot forbear at this point from expressing my amazement that in the face of this retaliation—inevitable from the day that the Grundy tariff became a law and predicted by every competent observer at home and abroad—not one effective step to deal with it or to alleviate its consequences was taken or even proposed by the national administration. Of the steps now to be taken I shall be explicit. But here let us pause for a moment to consider permanent farm relief in its longer perspective. I am coming to the shorter perspective later on. I suggest the following permanent measures:

First, reorganization of the Department of Agriculture is necessary with the purpose of building up a program of national agricultural planning. The department has done many good things, but I know enough of the ways of government to know that the growth of a department is often irregular and haphazard. It is always easy to add to a department, for additions mean more jobs. Particularly with the Department of Agriculture, to cut away unnecessary functions, to eliminate useless jobs, and to redirect routine activities toward more fruitful purposes is a task that must and shall be undertaken.

Second, to put into effect a definite policy toward the planned use of land.

Third, to reduce farm taxation and to more equitably distribute their burden.

These three objectives are the sort that will require slow-moving development. They constitute a necessary building for the future.

In meeting the immediate problems of distress it is necessary to adopt quick-acting remedies. There is the immediate necessity for the better financing of farm mortgages in order to relieve the burden of excessive interest charges and the grim threat of foreclosure. Much work was done in the last Congress to extend and liquefy and pass on to the Federal Government a portion of the debts of railroads, of banks, of utilities and industry in general. Something in the nature of a gesture was made in the financing of urban and suburban homes. But practically nothing was done toward removing the menace of debt from farm homes.

It is my purpose to direct all the energies of which I am capable to definite projects to relieve that distress and specifically I am prepared to insist that Federal credit be extended to banks, insurance companies, loan companies or corporations that hold farm mortgages among their assets; but that these credits be made on the condition that every reasonable assistance be given to the mortgagers where the loans are sound, for the purpose of preventing foreclosure. And those conditions must be enforced. Lower interest rates and an extension of principal payments will save thousands of farms for their owners. And hand in hand with that we must give those who have lost the title to their farms—titles now held by institutions now seeking credit from governmental agencies—the preferred opportunity of getting their property back.

As a further immediate aid to agriculture we should repeal those provisions of law that compel the Federal Government to go into the market to purchase, to sell, to speculate in farm products, in a futile attempt to reduce farm surpluses. We should have such a planning of farm production as would reduce the surplus and make it unnecessary in later years to depend on dumping those surpluses abroad in order to support domestic prices. That result has been accomplished in other nations; why not in America?

Another immediate necessity is to provide a means of bringing about through government effort, a substantial reduction in the difference between the prices of things the farmer sells and the things the farmer buys. One way of correcting that disparity is by restoring international trade through tariff readjustments.

This tariff policy consists in large measure in negotiating agreements with individual countries, permitting them to sell goods to us, in return for which they will let us sell to them goods and crops which we produce. The effective application of that principle will restore the flow of international trade and the first result of that flow will be to assist substantially the American farmer in disposing of his surplus. But it is recognized that to take up the slack until international trade is completely restored—and that may mean some time, for we cannot put through a new tariff negotiation in a few years—we must devise means to provide for the farmer a benefit that will give him in the shortest possible time the equivalent of what the protected manufacturer gets from the tariff. Farmers put this in a single phrase: "We must make the tariff effective."

In the last few years many plans have been devised for achieving that object. None has been given a trial. Circumstances are so complex that no man can say, with definite assurance, that one plan is applicable to all crops, or even that one plan is better than another in relation to an individual crop. One fact I want to make clear with all possible emphasis. There is no reason to despair merely because defects have been found by some people in all these plans, or because some of them have been discarded by responsible leaders in favor of new plans. The fact that so much study and earnest investigation of this problem has been made from so many angles and by so many men is, in my opinion, grounds for assurance rather than despair. Such a wealth of information has been accumulated, so many possibilities explored, so many able minds enlisted, and more important still, so much education on the subject provided for and by farmers themselves, that the time has come when able and thoughtful leaders who have followed this development from the beginning are now focussing on the basic elements of the problem, the practical nature of its solution, and are ready to put the thing through.

Within the past year, many of our industrialists have come to the conclusion that since the great decline of our export trade, the chief hope of industrial rehabilitation lies in a workable and important method of dealing with farm surpluses. Support for the trial of some plan to put the tariff into effect seems to be found everywhere now.

It will be my purpose to compose the conflicting elements of these various plans, to gather the benefit of the long study and consideration of them, to coordinate efforts to the end that agreement may be reached upon the details of a distinct policy to restore agriculture to economic equality with other industry.

The purpose is clear. The requirement is obvious; it is to give that portion of the crop consumed in the United States a benefit equivalent to a tariff sufficient to give the farmers an adequate price.

The specifications of the plan, upon which most of the reasonable leaders of agriculture have agreed, seem to me to be as follows:

The plan must provide for the producer of staple surplus

commodities, such as wheat, cotton, corn (in the form of hogs) and tobacco, a tariff benefit over world prices which is equivalent to the benefit given by the tariff to industrial products, and that differential benefit must be applied so that the increase in the farm income purchasing and debt-paying power will not stimulate further production, additional production.

The plan must finance itself. Agriculture has at no time sought and does not seek any such access to the public treasury as was provided by the futile and costly attempts at price stabilization by the Federal Farm Board. It seeks only equality of opportunity and tariff productive industry.

The plan must not make use of any mechanism which would cause our European customers to retaliate on the ground of dumping. It must be based on making the tariff effective and direct in its operation.

The plan must make use of existing agencies, and, so far as possible, be decentralized in its administration so that the chief responsibility for its success will rest with the localities of this country rather than with created bureaucratic machinery in Washington.

The plan must operate as nearly as possible on a cooperative basis and its effect must be to enhance and strengthen a cooperative movement. It should, moreover, be constituted so that it can be withdrawn whenever the emergency is passed and whenever normal foreign markets have been reestablished.

The plan must be, insofar as possible, voluntary. I like the idea that the plan should not be put into operation unless it has the support of a large, reasonable proportion of the producers of the exportable commodities, to which it is to apply. It must be so organized that the benefits will go to the man who participates.

These seem to me to be the essential specifications of a workable plan. In determining the details necessary to the solution of so vast a problem it goes without saying that many minds must meet and many persons work together. Such cooperation must of necessity come from those who have had the widest experience with the problem and who enjoy to the greatest degree the confidence of the farmers of the nation. Without in any sense seeking to avoid responsibility, I shall avail myself of the widest possible range of such assistance. I am confident of a solution, for the specification, for the first time in our economic history, is clear.

VIII

The Power Issue

THE POWER ISSUE, where vigorously handled in the public interest, means abundant and cheaper power for American industry, reduced rates and increased use in millions of urban and rural homes—to say little of the preservation of our waterpower resources in coordination with flood control, reclamation and irrigation. The American people have a vital stake in the proper handling of this issue.

Let us be clear at the outset that the liberty of individuals to carry on their business should not be abrogated unless the larger interests of the many are concerned. It is the purpose of government to see that not only the legitimate interests of the few are protected but that the welfare and rights of the many are conserved. These are the principles which must be remembered in any consideration of this question. This, I take it, is sound government—not politics. Those are the essential basic conditions under which government can be of service.

Power has been discussed so much in complex language,

in terms which only a lawyer can understand, or in figures which only accountants can understand, that there is need for bringing it back into the realm of simple, honest terms understood by millions of our citizens.

This is particularly true because there has not only been lack of information, and information difficult to understand, but there has been in the past few years, as the Federal Trade Commission has shown, a systematic, subtle, deliberate and unprincipled campaign of misinformation, of propaganda, and, if I may use the words, of lies and falsehood.

The spreading of this information has been bought and paid for by certain great private utility corporations. It has permeated the schools, the editorial columns of newspapers, the activities of political parties and the printed literature in our book stores.

A false public policy has been spread through the land, through the use of every means, from the innocent school teacher down to others far less innocent.

Let us go back to the beginning of the subject. What is a public utility? Let me take you back three hundred years to King James of England. The reign of this King is remembered for many great events, two of them in particular: he gave us a great translation of the Bible and the inception of a great public policy. It was in the days when Shakespeare was writing and when the English were settling Jamestown, that a public outcry arose in England from travellers who sought to cross the deeper streams by means of ferryboats.

Obviously these ferries, which were needed to connect the highway on one side with the highway on the other, were limited to specific points. They were, therefore, monopolistic in their nature.

The ferryboat operators, because of their privileged position, had the chance to charge whatever the traffic would bear, and bad service and high rates had the effect of forcing much trade and travel into long detours or to the dangers of attempting to ford the streams. The greed and avarice of some of these ferryboat owners remained a public issue for many years until in the days of Lord Hale a statement of public policy was set forth by the great Chief Justice.

The law lord said that the ferrymen's business was quite different from other businesses, that the ferry business was, in fact, vested with a public character, that to charge excessive rates was to set up obstacles to public use, and that the rendering of good service was a necessary and public responsibility.

"Each ferry," said Lord Hale, "ought to be under a public regulation, to wit, that it give attendance at due time, a boat in due order and take but reasonable toll."

In those simple words Lord Hale laid down a standard which, in theory at least, has been the definition of common law with respect to the authority of government over public utilities from that day to this.

With the advance of civilization, many other necessities of a monopolistic character have been added to the list of public utilities—such necessities as railroads, street railways, pipelines and the distribution of gas and electricity. This principle was accepted, firmly established, and became a basic part of our theory of government.

The next problem was how to be sure that the services of this kind should be satisfactory and cheap enough, while, at the same time, making possible the safe investment of new capital.

For more than two centuries the protection of the public was through legislative action, but, with the growth of the use of public utilities of all kinds, a more convenient, direct and scientific method had to be adopted—a method which we know as control and regulation by public service or public utility commission.

Let me make it clear that I have no objection to the method of control through a public service commission. It is the proper way for the people themselves to protect their interests. In practice, however, it has in many instances departed from its proper sphere of action and also from its theory of responsibility. It is an undeniable fact that in our modern American practice the public service commissions of many states have often failed to live up to the high purpose for which they were created. In many instances their selection has been obtained by the public utility corporations themselves. These corporations have often influenced, to the prejudice of the public, the actions of public service commissions. Moreover, some of the commissions have, either through deliberate intent or through sheer inertia, adopted a theory of their duties wholly at variance with the original object for which they were created.

For example, when I became Governor of the State of New York I found that the Public Service Commission of the State had adopted the unwarranted and unsound view that its sole function was to act as an arbitrator or a court between the public on one side and the utility corporations on the other.

I thereupon laid down a principle which created horror and havoc among the Insulls and other magnates of that type. I declared that the Public Service Commission is not a mere judicial body to act solely as umpire between complaining consumer or complaining investor on the one hand and the great public utility system on the other. I declared that, as the agent of the Legislature, it had delegated authority to act as the agent of the public; that it is not a mere arbitrator between the people and the public utilities, but was created for the purpose of seeing that the utilities do two things—give service and charge reasonable rates. I told them that, in performing this function, it must be as agent of the public upon its own initiative as well as upon petition to investigate the acts of public utilities relative to service and rules and to enforce adequate service and reasonable rates.

The regulation commission must be a tribune of the people, putting its engineering, accounting and legal resources into real use for the purpose of getting the facts and doing justice to both the consumers and the investors in public utilities. This means positive and active protection of the public against private greed.

So much for the simple, clear, definite theory of regulation—a theory which today is honored more in the breach than in the observance.

Now I come to another principle which, in spite of being befogged by many utility companies and, I am sorry to say, by many of our courts as well, is nevertheless clear and simple at root. The ferryman of old, under King James, through regulation and control of the government was compelled to give good service for a fair return on his labor and his property. But today the public utilities have found ways of paying to themselves inordinate and unreasonable profits and overcapitalizing their equipment by as much as even ten times the sums they have put into it.

The condition of overcapitalization does not need any elaborate presentation of figures for proof. I merely ask you to remember a few facts in connection with it. Senator Norris, using the facts of the Federal Trade Commission, in a speech in the Senate last year, pointed out the overcapitalization of many companies by name in definite figures and summed up the discussion by setting forth in round numbers to the extent of five hundred and twenty millions of dollars the amounts these main companies had been found to have overcapitalized.

This means that the people of the United States were called upon to supply profits upon this amount of watered stock. It meant that someone was deriving profits from the capitalization into which they had put no substantial capital. It meant that the people had to pay these unjust profits through higher rates.

As Senator Norris said: "Just try to comprehend what this means. With the investigation only partially finished, the Federal Trade Commission has disclosed 'write-ups' [water] . . . upon which the people must pay a profit for all time. . . . Unless some change is made in public authority, it must be paid forever."

Let us consider for a moment the vast importance of the American utilities in our economic life—and in this I am not including the railroads and other transportation companies. The utility industry in 1931 collected over four billion dollars from the users of electricity, gas, telephone and telegraph. This means an average of one hundred and thirty-three dollars for every family in the United States.

According to the figures of the industry itself, the American public has invested nearly twenty-three billion dollars in public utilities, again excluding the railroads. Of this sum nearly eight billions were invested in the electric light and power industry alone during the five years that preceded the stock market collapse in 1929.

Compare this with the eleven billions invested in railroads, nine billions in farm mortgages and with the national debt of the United States itself, which was something slightly less than this investment in public utilities. You will readily see that this "lusty child" of the United States needs to be kept very closely under the watchful eye of its parent—the people.

But these figures do not measure the human importance of electric power in our present social order. Electricity is no longer a luxury; it is a definite necessity. It lights our homes, our places of work, our streets; it turns the wheels of our transportation and our factories.

It can relieve the drudgery of the housewife and lift a great burden from the shoulders of the farmer. It has not done so yet. We are backward in the use of electricity in our homes and on our farms. In Canada the average home uses twice as much electric power per family as we do in the United States. What prevents us from taking advantage of this great economic and human agency?

It is not because we lack undeveloped water-power or unclaimed supplies of coal and oil. The reason we cannot take advantage of our own possibilities is because many selfish interests in control of light and power industries have not been sufficiently far-sighted to establish rates low enough to encourage widespread public use. The price you pay for your utility service is a determining factor in your use of it.

Low prices to the domestic consumer will result in his using far more electrical appliances than he does today.

Through lack of vigilance in state capitals and in the national government, we have allowed many utility companies to get around the common law, to capitalize themselves without regard to actual investment made in property, to pyramid capital through holding companies and without restraint of law, to sell billions of dollars of securities which the public have been falsely led into believing were properly supervised by the government itself.

The crash of the "Insull Empire" has given an excellent example of the truth. The great "Insull monstrosity," made up of a group of holding and investment companies and exercising control over hundreds of operating companies, had distributed securities among hundreds of thousands of investors, and had taken their money to an amount running over one and a half billion dollars. The Insull organization grew until it reached a position where it was an important factor in the lives of millions of people. The name was magic. The investing public did not realize then, as it does now, that the methods used in building up these holding companies were wholly contrary to every sound public policy. They did not realize that there had been arbitrary write-ups of assets, inflation of vast capital accounts; they did not realize that there had been excessive prices paid for property acquired; they did not realize that the expense of financing had been capitalized; they did not realize that payments of dividends had been made out of capital.

They did not realize that some subsidiaries had been milked and milked to keep alive the weaker sisters in the great chain. They did not realize that there had been borrowings and lendings, an interchange of assets, of liabilities and of capital between the component parts of the whole. They did not realize that all these conditions necessitated terrific overcharges for service by these corporations.

The Insull failure has opened our eyes. It shows us that the development of these financial monstrosities was such as to compel ultimate ruin; that practices had been indulged in that suggest the old days of railroad wildcatting; that private manipulation had out-smarted the slow-moving power of government.

As always, the public paid and paid dearly. As always, the public is beginning to understand the need for reform after that same public has been fleeced.

The new deal for the American people can be applied

very definitely to the relationship between the electric utilities on the one side and the consumer and investor on the
other.

True regulation is for the equal benefit of the consumer
and the investor, and the only man who will suffer from
true regulation is the speculator or the unscrupulous promoter who levies tribute equally from the man who buys
the service and from the man who invests his savings in this
great industry.

I seek to protect both the consumer and the investor. To
that end I propose, as I have in the past, the following remedies on the part of the government for the regulation and
control of public utilities engaged in the power business
and corporations and companies relating thereto:

1. Full publicity as to all capital issues of stock, bonds
   and other securities, liabilities and indebtedness, and
   capital investment, and frequent information as to
   gross and net earnings.

2. Publicity on stock ownership of stocks and bonds
   and other securities, including the stock and other interest of all officers and directors.

3. Publicity with respect to all inter-company contracts and services and interchange of power.

4. Regulation and control of holding companies by
   the Federal power commission and the same publicity

with regard to such holding companies as provided by the operating companies.

5. Cooperation of the Federal power commission with public utilities commissions of the several states, obtaining information and data pertaining to the regulation and control of such public utilities.

6. Regulation and control of the issue of stocks and bonds and other securities on the principle of prudent investment only.

7. Abolishing by law the reproduction of cost theory for rate making and establishing in place of it the actual money, prudent investment principle as the basis of rate making.

8. Legislation making it a crime to publish or circulate false or deceptive matter relating to public utilities.

The proper relationship of the government to the development through government itself of power resources and power manufacture is clear enough if the fundamental rights of the individual and the government are kept in mind. I do not hold with those who advocate government ownership or government operation of all utilities. As a broad general rule, the development of utilities should remain, with certain exceptions, a function for private initiative and private capital.

But the exceptions are of vital importance, local, state and national, and I believe that the overwhelming majority of the people of this country agree with me.

Again, we must go back to first principles; a utility is in most cases a monopoly, and it is by no means possible in every case for government to insure from mere inspection, supervision and regulation that the public should get a fair deal—in other words, to insure adequate service and reasonable rates.

Therefore I lay down the following principle: that where a community or a district is not satisfied with the service rendered or the rates charged by a private utility, it has the undeniable right as one of its functions of government, one of its functions of home rule, to set up, after a fair referendum has been taken, its own governmentally owned and operated service.

This right has been recognized in most of the states of the Union. Its general recognition by every state will hasten the day of better service and lower rates.

It is perfectly clear to me and to every thinking citizen that no community which is sure that it is now being served well and at reasonable rates by a private utility company will seek to build or operate its own plant. But on the other hand, the very fact that a community, by vote of the electorate, may create a yardstick of its own, will in most cases guarantee good service and low rates. This is the principle that applies to communities. I would apply the same principles to the Federal and State governments.

State-owned or Federal-owned power sites can and

should properly be developed by government itself. When so developed, private capital should be given the first opportunity to transmit and distribute the power on the basis of the best service and the lowest rates to give a reasonable profit only.

The nation, through its Federal Government, has sovereignty over vast waterpower resources in many parts of the United States. A very few of them are in progress of development. A few more are in the stage of blueprints and many others have not even been surveyed.

We have undertaken the development of the Boulder Dam on the Colorado River. The power will be sold by the United States Government at a cost that will return the government investment with four percent interest in fifty years. States and municipalities were given a prior right to contract the power so generated. Long before that we undertook the development at Muscle Shoals. We have spent millions on this project. The 1930 session of the Congress passed the bill introduced by Senator Norris for public operation of Muscle Shoals. The bill was vetoed.

There are two other great developments to be undertaken by the Federal Government. One is the Columbia River in the Northwest. This vast water power can be of incalculable value to this whole section of the country. One is the St. Lawrence River in the Northeast. Together with Muscle Shoals in the Southeast and Boulder Dam in the Southwest, we shall forever have a national yardstick to prevent extortion against the public and to encourage the wider use of that servant of the people—electricity.

As an important part of this policy, the natural hydro-electric power resources belonging to the people should remain forever in their possession. This policy is as radical as American liberty, as radical as the Constitution of the United States. Never shall the Federal Government part with its sovereignty and control over its power resources while I am President of the United States.

IX

THE RAILROADS

THE DEVELOPMENT OF the public utilities is, particularly at this present stage of our economic life, the development of the nation. In the building of the West, for example, that great public utility—the railroad—was the dominant factor. For ninety years the railroads have been the means of tying us all together in national unity.

In this development we have seen great heroism, great faith and, unfortunately, also great injustice. When the railroad first stretched out across the Western plains it was regarded as a miracle, challenging the imagination of the people. Later there came an age when the railroads, controlled by men who unfortunately did not recognize the large public interest at stake, were regarded by those same people as an octopus, crushing out their life and sapping their substance.

But that day has passed. The railroad is becoming a servant of the people, largely owned by the people themselves. It is this new relationship of the railroad that should guide our consideration of its problems. The railroad that was first a miracle, next a sinister threat, has now become a part of our national economic life. We are now concerned about its preservation.

The problem of the railroads is the problem of each and every one of us. No single economic activity enters into the life of every individual so much as do these great carriers. It is well to pause a moment and examine the extent of that interest.

The issue should be thought through in terms of individual men and women. A railroad indirectly affects everyone within its vast territory. Directly it affects three great groups.

First, there are its owners. They are not, as too many still suppose, great railway magnates sitting in luxurious offices and clubs. They are the people throughout the country who have a savings bank account or an insurance policy, or, in some measure, an ordinary checking account. Figures, though they may be dull, nevertheless do talk.

There are more than eleven billions of railroad bonds outstanding—about half as many, in fact, as there are United States Government obligations. Nearly five billions of them are owned by savings banks and insurance companies—which means that they are owned by the millions of policy holders and savings bank depositors.

When you put money in the bank or pay an insurance premium, you are automatically buying an interest in the railroads.

Some two billion dollars more of railroad bonds are held by churches, hospitals, charitable organizations, colleges and similar institutions as endowment. The remaining bonds are scattered far and wide among a host of people whose life savings have been invested in this standard American industry.

Even railroad stocks are held in small units of a few shares here and there, by school teachers, doctors, salesmen, thrifty workmen. Experts in railroad finance know that perhaps thirty million people have a stake in these great American enterprises.

Next, there are the people who work in the railway systems, either directly on the lines or in the industries which furnish railway supplies. There are over one million seven hundred thousand railroad employees required to handle normal traffic, and to these must be added, in direct interest, hundreds of thousands of men who supply coal, forge rails, cut ties, manufacture rolling stock and contribute labor to maintain the systems.

Most numerous of all are the people who ride or ship goods over the steel highways. That includes about all of us.

There is no reason to disguise the fact that the railroads are in serious difficulties. And when so large a part of the American people have a direct cash stake in the situation, I take it that our job is neither to howl about a calamity nor gloss over the trouble, but patiently and carefully to get to the bottom of the situation, find out why the trouble exists and try to plan for a removal of the basic causes of that trouble.

I do not share the opinion that has been aired recently

that the railroads have served their purpose and are about to disappear. Capable students of American transportation do not support that view. As Professor Ripley of Harvard has pointed out, if you tried to carry all railroad freight by motor truck, you would have to have a fleet of trucks which would make a solid line, bumper to bumper, all the way from New York to San Francisco; or, to put it differently, you would have to have a ten-ton truck moving every thirty seconds over every mile of improved road in the United States.

Let us put it another way. In a normal year our railroads are called upon to transport over thirty million people one thousand miles and to transport four hundred and forty million tons of freight one thousand miles. No other machine is available to carry that load.

There is no danger of the railroads going out of business. They have a great economic place in the scheme of things for a good long time to come.

Why, then, the difficulty?

In the first place, we unbalanced the system of things. We built—properly—hundreds of thousands of miles of first-rate highways directly paralleling the railway tracks. These we paid for out of taxes or bond issues. Today many hundred busses and trucks engage in interstate commerce, using these rights of way for which they have made no investment.

You and I, in our annual tax bills, pay for most of the maintenance of the highways and interest charges on their construction. The motor vehicles pay only a small part. Naturally they can often haul passengers and freight at a relatively smaller overhead and capital, lower taxes and lower maintenance costs for their right of way.

Also we, the national government, allow them to operate free from many restrictions which would insure safety to the public and fair working conditions for labor. We should not give them any unfair competitive advantages over the rails.

We do not desire to put motor vehicle transportation out of its legitimate field of business, for it is a necessary and important part of our transportation systems; but motor transportation should be placed under the same Federal supervision as railroad transportation.

While thus forcing the railroads to meet unfair competition we have not only permitted but frequently required them to compete unreasonably with each other. In regulating the railroads we have preserved the policy that at all times, between principal points, there must be competing railroad systems. There is a great deal to be said for this policy, so long as there is traffic enough to support competing lines. So long as you have that traffic, the competition helps to insure efficiency.

But as the railroads have been allowed to increase their capacity far beyond traffic needs, the wastes of competition have become more and more insupportable. Now we face the issues: Shall we permit them—force them, in fact—to bankrupt each other? Or shall we permit them to consolidate and so to economize through reducing unprofitable services? In other words, shall we permit them to divide traffic and so eliminate some of the present wastes?

No solution is entirely attractive, because we have the problem of an overbuilt plant, or partially unemployed capital, a problem similar in its difficulty to that of unemployed labor. But a definite, sound public policy actually carried out will hasten improvement.

We can cut out some expensive deadwood in the shape of unnecessary or duplicated facilities. The public generally does not realize that thirty percent of railroad mileage carries only two percent of the freight and passenger traffic. This does not mean that all of this mileage can or ought to be scrapped. But it does suggest that a considerable amount of judicious pruning can gradually be done without public detriment.

Finally, there has been entirely too much maneuvering for position among the railroads themselves in the past ten years. We have had an epidemic of railroad holding companies whose financial operations were, to say the least, not generally beneficial to the orderly development of transportation. They were financial comets, free to rove through the system, spending other people's money in financial gambles and in acquiring side enterprises outside of the direct sphere of railroading. A great deal of money has been lost and a great deal of damage has been done by these companies.

All of the foregoing should indicate that one chief cause of the present railroad problem has been that typical cause of many of our problems, the entire absence of any national planning for the continuance and operation of this absolutely vital national utility.

The individual railroads should be regarded as parts of a national transportation service. This does not mean all should be under one management. Indeed, the principal doubt of the efficiency of consolidations has been caused by the repeated demonstration that a great railroad is made by good executives; and experience has shown that the mileage over which one manager can be effective is limited to a small fraction of our national mileage.

But it is necessary that a single railroad should have a recognized field of operation and a part to play in the entire national scheme of transportation. It is necessary that each rail service should fit into and be coordinated with other rail services and with other forms of transportation. Let it be noted that our postal service uses every variety of transport: rail, automobile, steamship and aeroplane; but it controls few of these vehicles.

We might well approach the railroad problem from a similar point of view—survey all our national transportation needs, determine the most efficient, economical means of transportation, and substitute a national policy for national lack of planning, and encourage that growth and expansion most healthful to the general welfare.

In common counsel and common purposes we shall find the corrective of a present unhappy tendency to look for dictators. The wisdom of many men can save us from the errors of supposed supermen.

To those who may shrink from any suggestion of a more vigorous and coherent public railroad program, I venture to point out that it has not been the existence but the lack of a public policy which has caused just criticism of railroad regulation.

The definite programs of the past—to stop rate wars, to prevent rebates and discriminations, to improve safety— these have all produced great public benefits and have saved the railroads from themselves. But in the post-war political drift and private mastery, we have too often fumbled rather than grappled with railroad problems.

I do not share the view that government regulation *per se* is responsible for any great amount of the present difficulties. Had this been true we should have known it long before the depression came.

In the words of one of the railway presidents, "there is no question whatever that the regulation of the railroads of the country has been in the public interest." Regulation, in fact, has protected the investors as well as patrons and I think that no enlightened man would care to go back to the old days when unregulated railroad operation landed one-third of the railroad mileage in receivership.

When the depression came, with its great loss of tonnage, the combined effect of uneconomic competition, unproductive and overextended mileage, imprudent financial adventures and frequently ill-advised management resulted in a situation where many railroads literally were unable to earn their interest charges.

The government then, through the Reconstruction Finance Corporation, undertook to tide over the emergency by freely lending money to the railroads, with a view to keeping them afloat.

I am glad to approve this policy—as an emergency measure—though I do not go along with many of the methods. As far as it goes the policy is a good one. We had far too great a stake in the situation to allow a general smash-up.

I shall continue the policy of trying to prevent receiverships. But I do not believe that this is more than a stop-gap. Lending money is all right if—and only if—you put your borrower in a position where he can pay you back.

The criticism, I think, is well founded that the government did not follow through with a well-considered program of putting the railroads back upon their feet. And certainly when the railroads applied for cash the government was at least entitled to make the kind of requirement which a private banker would make under similar circumstances to protect his interest. The government, in lending public money, is entitled and should make sure to protect the public interest.

Further, when mere loans cannot clear up the situation, the necessary readjustments ought to be provided as a part of the plan of lending. In its railroad relief, as elsewhere, the last administration has lent money, not in accordance with a plan for relieving fundamental difficulties, but only with the hope that within a year or two the depression would end.

Facing the facts squarely, we may as well realize, first rather than last, the fundamental issues.

Railroad securities in general must not be allowed to drift into default. The damage done to savings banks, insurance companies, and fiduciary institutions generally would be too great.

But let me make clear that the extension of government credit will be largely wasted unless with it there are adopted the constructive measures required to clean house. In individual railroads these turn on the financial conditions peculiar to each case. In certain situations where fixed charges impose an unsound overstrain, these charges must be reduced.

In general, corrective measures must be adopted making for a sounder financial structure along the lines I will now enumerate. Unless the underlying conditions are recognized we are wasting our time and our money.

Concretely, I advocate:

First—That the government announce its intention to stand back of the railroads for a specific period; its help being definitely conditioned upon acceptance by the railroads of such requirements as may in individual cases be found necessary to readjust top-heavy financial structures through appropriate scaling-down of fixed charges. I propose the preliminary development of a national transportation policy with the aid of legislative and administrative officials and representatives of all interests most deeply concerned with the welfare and service of the railroads, including investors, labor, shippers and passengers. I propose that in the application of this policy to the railroads the Reconstruction Finance Corporation, working with the Interstate Commerce

Commission, share the work of planning the reorganization or readjustment for the protection of all concerned.

And I also propose that when such plans have been worked out, the same agencies shall indicate a specified period of support to see the railroads through in the carrying out of these plans.

Second—To aid in the rehabilitation of roads unable to meet the present unprecedented strain, or that may succumb to past or future mismanagement, I propose a thorough overhauling of the Federal laws affecting railroad receiverships, and indeed of all kinds of public utility receiverships. As they now stand they suggest Mr. Dooley's favorite dictum that they are arranged so that every member of the bar may get his fair share of the assets. There is an urgent need to eliminate a multiplicity of court actions, a maze of judicial steps, a long period of business chaos and a staggering expense allowed to lawyers, receivers, committees and so on. Included in this revised procedure should be a provision by which the interests of security holders and creditors shall be more thoroughly protected at all points against irresponsible or self-interested reorganization managers.

Third—I advocate the regulation of competing motor carriers, by the Interstate Commerce Commission. Where rail service should be supplemented by motor service to promote the public interest, the railroads should be permitted in this manner to extend their transportation facilities. They should be encouraged to modernize and adapt their plant to the new needs of a changing world.

Fourth—I believe that the policy of enforced competition between railroads can be carried to unnecessary lengths. For example, the Interstate Commerce Commission should be relieved of requiring competition where traffic is insufficient to support competing lines, recognizing the clear and absolute responsibility for protecting the public against any abuses of monopolistic power. Likewise, I believe that the elimination of non-paying mileage should be encouraged wherever the transportation needs of the community affected can be otherwise adequately met.

Fifth—Proposed consolidations of railroads which are lawful and in the public interest should be pressed to a conclusion. At the same time the provisions of the law should be revised in line with the policies here proposed and with repeated suggestions of the Interstate Commerce Commission and of representatives of shippers, carriers and their employees, to insure further protection of public and private interests involved. There should be clearer definitions of the objects, powers and duties of the Commission in promoting and safeguarding all the interrelated particular interests comprehended within the public interest. Those who have invested their money or their lives in the service of the railroad; those who are dependent upon its service to buy or sell goods; those who rely upon it for the preservation of communities into which they have built their lives—all have vital interests which must be further safeguarded.

All of the appropriate agencies of the Federal and state governments should have a part in a national effort to improve the health of these great arteries of commerce.

Sixth—So-called "railroad holding companies" should be definitely put under the regulation and control of the Interstate Commerce Commission in like manner as railroads themselves. We cannot let our fundamental policies be blocked by screens of corporate complexities.

Finally we must realize that government encouragement and cooperation, more than mere restriction and repression, will produce lasting improvement in transportation conditions. The economy and efficiency of railroad operation will depend upon the capacity of railroad management and its freedom from undue burdens and restraints when it is balanced by the acceptance of public responsibilities. It will also depend in large measure upon the competence and morale of railroad employees—perhaps the largest body of skilled workers functioning as a unit in our industrial life.

Transportation is not a mechanized service. It is a service of human beings whose lives are worthy of even more intelligent care than that necessary to preserve the physical mechanisms which they operate. And it is clear to me that all the men and women who are employed in our great transportation systems are entitled to the highest possible wages that the industry can afford to pay.

We must pay the fair cost of this transportation, which is a small fraction of the selling price of commodities. We cannot burden our producers or restrict their markets by excessive costs of transportation.

As a soundly devised public policy reaches its fruition, railway security owners may expect greater certainty of fair but not excessive return; the public may reasonably expect lower rates; labor may reasonably anticipate security in properly compensated work.

I do not fear any government action which will relieve railway managements of performing their responsibilities. It is well to remember that the actual railway operators are not the owners of the railroads, nor the major users of railway services, and today they only command access to capital on the basis of their ability to protect capital.

Their position now depends, as it ought to, on their being able to do their job well. We are entitled to demand, and I think they would be the first to concede, that they give a management which is sound, economic and skillful; that they do not use their positions as financial stewards to further personal desires for gain or power. They are, in reality, public servants who are entitled to every assistance from the government, but held to high standards of accountability.

The new situation today is that most of our railroads throughout the nation are failing month by month to earn the fixed charges on their existing debts. Continuance of this failure means bankruptcy.

I want the railroads to stand on their own feet, ultimately to reduce their debts instead of increasing them and thereby save not only a great national investment, but also the safety of employment of nearly two million American railway workers. The maintenance of their standard of living is a vital concern of the national government.

In the great task of reordering the dislocated economics of America we must constantly strive for three ends:

efficiency of service, safety of financial structure and permanence of employment. The railroad mesh is the warp on which our economic web is largely fashioned. It has made a continent into a nation. It has saved us from splitting, like Europe, into small, clashing units; it made possible the rise of the West; it is our service of supply. These are not matters of private concern; they have no place in the excesses of speculation, nor can they be allowed to become springboards of financial ambition.

Such readjustments as must be made should be so made that they will not have to be done again; and the system must become, as it should be, secure, serviceable, national.

X

THE TARIFF

FROM THE BEGINNING of our government one of the most difficult questions in our economic life has been the tariff. But it is a fact that it is now so interwoven with our whole economic structure, and that structure is so intricate and delicate a pattern of causes and effects, that tariff revision must be undertaken with scrupulous care, and only on the basis of established facts.

Yet there is scarcely a major problem in our national life—agriculture, industry and labor, merchant marine, international debt and even disarmament—that does not involve the question of the tariff.

A tariff is a tax on certain goods passing from the producer to the consumer. It is laid on these goods rather than other similar ones because they originate abroad. This is obviously protection for the producers of competing goods at home. Peasants who live at lower levels than our farmers, workers who are sweated to reduce costs, ought not to determine prices for American-made goods. There are standards which we desire to set for ourselves. Tariffs should be high enough to maintain living standards which we set for ourselves. But if they are higher they become a particularly vicious kind of direct tax which is laid doubly on the consumer. Not only are the prices of foreign goods raised, but those of domestic goods also.

In the past the proposition has been laid down with great boldness that high tariffs interfere only slightly, if at all, with our export or our import trade; that they are necessary to the success of agriculture and afford essential farm relief; that they do not interfere with the payments of debts to us—that they are absolutely necessary to the economic formula for the abolition of poverty.

The experience of the last four years has unhappily demonstrated the error of every single one of these propositions; that every one of them has been one of the effective causes of the present depression, and finally that no substantial progress of recovery from the depression, either here or abroad, can be had without forthright recognition of these errors.

I ask effective action to reverse these disastrous policies.

The false promises of prosperity of the recent past were based on the assertion that although our agriculture was producing a surplus far in excess of our power to consume, and although, due to the mass and automatic machine production today, our industrial production had also passed far beyond the point of domestic consumption, nevertheless we should press forward to increase industrial production as the only means of maintaining profitable employment. It was insisted that although we could not consume these things at home, there was an unlimited market for our rapidly increasing surplus in export trade, and that we were on the verge of the greatest commercial expansion in history.

But when later confronted by the difficult question as to how foreign nations would pay their debts to us, and pay also for the increasing surplus it was proposed to sell to them, when by almost prohibitive tariffs the world commerce in goods was blocked, the astounding suggestion was ventured that we should finance our export by loans to "backward and crippled countries"—coupled with the reaffirmation that high tariffs would not interfere with the repayment of such loans.

Ostensibly for the purpose of enacting legislation for the relief of agriculture, the Congress was called into special session. The disastrous fruit of that session was the notorious and indefensible Grundy-Smoot-Hawley Tariff. The net result was a barbed wire entanglement against our economic contacts with the world at large.

As to the much heralded purpose of that special session, the result was a ghastly jest. This was so for several reasons: the principal cash crops of our farms are produced much in excess of our requirements; no tariff on the surplus crop, no matter how high the wall, has the slightest effect in raising the domestic price of that crop; the producers of these crops are as effectively thrust outside the protection of our tariff as if there was no tariff at all. But the tariff does protect the price of our industrial products and raises them above world prices—as the farmer with increasing bitterness has come to realize, he sells on a free-trade basis, but buys in a protected market. The higher industrial tariffs go, the greater is the farmer's burden.

The first effect of the Grundy Tariff was to increase or sustain the cost of all that agriculture buys. But the harm to our whole agricultural population did not stop there. Under recent world conditions, the Grundy Tariff, by gradually impairing the export markets for our farm surplus, resulted in a tremendous decrease in the price of all the farmer sells. The result of both these forces was practically to cut in half the pre-war purchasing power of American agriculture. The things the farmer buys now cost nine percent above pre-war prices; the things that the farmer sells are forty-three percent below pre-war prices. The farmer is hit both ways in consequence of the tariff. It increases the price of what he buys and, by restricting the foreign market that controls the price of his products, reduces his returns from what he sells.

The destructive effect of the Grundy Tariff has not been confined to agriculture. It has ruined our export trade in industrial products as well. Industry, with its foreign trade cut off, naturally began to look to the home market—a market supplied for the greater part by farm families. But when industry turned its eyes to the home market, it found that the Grundy Tariff had reduced the buying power of the farmer.

Deprived of any American market, the other industrial nations, in order to support their own industries and take care of their own unemployment problems, had to find new outlets. In this quest they took to trade agreements with countries other than ourselves. They also undertook the preservation of their own domestic markets against importations, by trade restrictions of all kinds. An almost frantic movement toward self-contained nationalism began. The direct result was a series of retaliatory and defensive measures in the shape of tariffs, embargos, import quotas and international arrangements.

Almost immediately international commerce began to languish, and especially the export markets for our industrial and agricultural surpluses began to disappear. The Grundy bill was passed in June, 1930; in that month our exports were three hundred and ninety-four million dollars in value and our imports two hundred and fifty millions. In an almost uninterrupted decline, this foreign trade dropped away so that, two years later, in June, 1932, our exports were worth one hundred and fifteen millions and our imports seventy-eight millions. These facts speak for themselves.

In 1929, a year before the enactment of the Grundy Tariff, we exported fifty-four and eight-tenths percent of all the cotton produced in the United States, more than one half. This means that in 1929 every other row of cotton produced was sold abroad. Of wheat, seventeen and nine-tenths percent was exported, though the foreign sales were largely sacrificed. And so with the grower of rye, who was able to dispose of twenty and nine-tenths percent of his crop to foreign markets. The grower of leaf tobacco had a stake of forty-one and two-tenths percent of his income overseas. One-third of the lard in this country was exported in that year; this concerns the corn grower, for corn is exported in the form of lard.

The ink on the Grundy bill was hardly dry before the foreign markets commenced their program of retaliation. Brick against brick they built their walls against us. They learned their lesson from us. "The villainy you teach me I shall practice."

While the Grundy bill was before the Congress, our State Department received one hundred and sixty protests from thirty-three nations, many of whom after the passage of the bill erected their own tariff walls to the detriment or destruction of much of our export trade.

What was the result? In two years, 1930 to May, 1932, American manufacturers established two hundred and fifty-eight factories in foreign countries to escape the penalty on the introduction of American-made goods—forty-eight of these were in Europe, twelve in Latin America, twenty-eight in the Far East and seventy-one in Canada. Every week of 1932 had seen four American factories moving to Canada.

Premier Bennett, of the Dominion, was reported to have said in a speech that "a factory is moving every day of the year from the United States to Canada" and assured those at the recent conference at Ottawa that by the arrangements made there Great Britain and her Colonies would take from Canada two hundred and fifty billions of trade which would otherwise go to the United States.

This puts more men on the street here, men who had been employed in the factories that moved to Canada.

There was a secondary and perhaps even more disastrous effect of this tariff. Billions of dollars of debts are due to this country from abroad. If the debtor nations cannot export goods and services, they must try to pay gold. We started such a drain on the gold reserves of the principal commercial countries as to force practically all of them off the gold standard. What has happened? The value of the money of each of these countries, relative to the value of the dollar, declined alarmingly. It took more Argentine pesos to buy an American plow. It took more English shillings to buy an American bushel of wheat or bale of cotton.

They could not buy our goods with their money. These goods were thrown back on our markets, and prices fell still more.

Summing up, the Grundy Tariff has largely extinguished the export markets for our industrial and our farm supplies; it has prevented the payment of public and private debts to us and the interest thereon, increasing our taxation to meet the expense of our government, and, finally, it has driven our factories abroad.

The process still continues. But unless this process is reversed throughout the world, there is no hope for full economic recovery or for true prosperity in the United States.

The essential trouble is that the past leaders of the nation thought they had a good patent in the doctrine of unscalable tariff walls and that no other nation could use the idea. Either the patent has expired—or it never was any good—or else all other nations have infringed and there is no court of appeal.

Do not ever expect the authors of this scheme to admit that it was a stupid, blundering idea. On the contrary, they adopted the boldest alibi, with regard to it, in the history of politics. They sought to avoid all responsibility for mismanagement by blaming the foreign victims for their economic blundering. They said and they still say that all our troubles come from abroad, that our past administration is not to be held to answer. This excuse is a classic of impertinence. If ever a condition was directly traceable to two specific American-made causes, it is the depression of this country and the world. These two causes are interrelated.

The second one, in the point of time, is this Grundy Tariff. The first one is the fact that by improvident loans to "backward and crippled countries" we financed practically our entire export trade and payment of interest and principal to us by our debtors. Thus in part we even financed the payment of German reparations.

When we began to diminish that financing in 1929, the economic structure of the world began to totter. When, in 1930, we imposed the Grundy Tariff, the tottering structure crumbled.

What can be done now?

We can create a competitive tariff, which means one which will put American producers on a market equality with their foreign competitors—one that equalizes the difference in the cost of production—not a prohibitory tariff back of which producers can combine to practice extortion upon the American public.

I appreciate that the doctrine thus announced is not

widely different from that preached by statesmen and politicians who have been in power in this country. I know that the theory professed by them has been that the tariff should equalize the difference in the cost of production, which for all practical purposes does not exceed labor cost as between this country and competitive countries—but I know that in practice this theory is utterly disregarded. The rates are imposed far in excess of any such differences, looking to the total exclusion of imports—prohibitory rates.

Instances without number to show the pious professions of those who have controlled the destiny of our nation, and the actual performance under that leadership, could be cited from the debates on the Grundy Tariff.

The outrageously excessive rates in that bill, as it became law, must come down. But we should not lower them below the point indicated. Such revision of the tariff will injure no legitimate interest. Labor need have no apprehension concerning such a course, for labor knows, by long and bitter experience, that the highly protected industries pay not one penny higher wages than the unprotected industries such as the automobile industry.

How is this reduction to be accomplished?

By international negotiation as the first and most desirable method, in view of present world conditions; by consenting to reduce to some extent some of our duties in order to secure a lowering of foreign walls that a larger surplus may be admitted from abroad.

It is worth remembering that President McKinley, in his last public address in 1901, said: "The period of exclusion is past. The period of expansion of our trade and commerce is the present problem. Reciprocal treaties are in harmony with the spirit of the time; measures of retaliation are not."

I have none of the fear that possesses some timorous minds that we should get the worst of it in such reciprocal arrangements. I ask if you have lost faith in our Yankee tradition of good old-fashioned trading? Do you believe that our early instincts for successful barter have atrophied or degenerated? I do not think so. There cannot and shall not be any foreign dictation of our tariff policies.

I propose to accomplish the necessary reduction through the agency of the Tariff Commission.

One of the most deplorable features of tariff legislation is the log-rolling by which it has been effected in the past. Perfectly indefensible rates are introduced through an understanding usually implied rather than understood among members of Congress, each of whom is interested in one or more of such. It is a case of you scratch my back and I will scratch yours. This evil must be recognized by even the most ardent supporter of the theory of protection.

To avoid this, as well as other evils in tariff making, a Democratic Congress in 1916 passed and a Democratic President approved a bill creating the bi-partisan tariff commission, charged with the duty of supplying the Congress with accurate and full information upon which to base tariff rates. It functioned as a scientific body until 1922, when by the incorporation of the so-called flexible provisions of the act of that year, it was transferred into a political body.

Under these provisions, reenacted in the Grundy Tariff of 1930, the Commission reports not to the Congress but to the President, who is empowered upon its recommendation to raise or lower the tariff rates by as much as fifty percent. How ineffective this method of removing from the tariff some of its inequities—a wag said, "its iniquities"—I need not detail.

At the last session of Congress, by the practically unanimous action of the Democrats of both houses, aided by liberal-minded Republicans, a bill was passed, but vetoed by the President, which, for the purpose of preventing log-rolling, provided that a report having been made on a particular item, with recommendation as to the rate of duty it ought to bear, a measure to make effective such rate could not include any other item not directly affected by the change proposed. In that way each particular tariff rate proposed would be judged upon its merits alone.

Another feature of this bill, designed to obviate log-rolling, contemplated the appointment of a public counsel, who should be heard on all applications for changes in rates before the Commission, on the one hand from increases sought by producers, often greedy, or from decreases asked by importers, equally actuated by selfish motives, or by others seeking such reductions. I hope some such change may be speedily enacted.

I am confident that under such a system rates would be adopted generally so reasonable that there would be very little opportunity for criticism or even cavilling as to them.

Despite the efforts repeated in every political campaign

to stigmatize the Democratic party as a free-trade party, there has never been a tariff act passed since the government came into existence in which the duties were not levied with a view to giving the American producer an advantage over his foreign competitor. And I think that you will agree with me that the difference today between the two major parties on the subject of the tariff is that the Republican party would put duties so high as to make them practically prohibitive. The Democratic party will put them as low as the preservation of American industry will permit.

I do not expect that the tariff will disappear as a political issue for some time to come, but I do expect that its modification according to the principles I have briefed will so clearly show its advantages to the nation as a whole that the discussion of it will devolve upon its more scientific application.

XI

JUDICIAL REFORM

EVERY GOVERNMENT POLICY should first be laid against the specification of the greatest good for the greatest number of individual men and women. Thus it is that matters which are not the direct responsibility of the Federal Government should often be matters of concern to it. Support and help should be given to national movements and impetus to trends which will give us a better government. So it is well to consider the points where government most closely touches the individual whether it happens to be a Federal function or not. One of them, assuredly, is justice; and from the manner in which he receives justice does the average citizen himself judge government, be it local, state or national.

It is unnecessary to take time in establishing the fact that the administration of justice is generally unpopular with the people of this country. Growing complaint with the law's injustices, delays and costs has to a great extent characterized every generation. The present one is no exception, but at the present time the problem rises into significance beyond the mere stage of dissatisfaction. It becomes a public problem of great importance.

Speedy and efficient justice is no more necessary to the individual in such vast communities as New York or Chicago than it is in the smaller places, but in the large communities it should be placed as soon as possible on a par of importance with health, sanitation and police protection if we are to give adequate government to the great masses of our citizens.

It is a matter of common knowledge that justice has not been adequately provided. Moreover, in a time of economic distress such as this, the multiplication of legal actions involving debts increases. The necessity for relief is accentuated.

It is impossible and unnecessary to consider here the extent to which this situation is caused by technical difficulty. It may be taken for granted that most of it is due to the fact that the rules of the legal game are such that in the absence of very strong administrative control it will be used not for a direct search for the truth but to permit such legal maneuvers as will further the interests of those who do not want the truth to be found.

The jury trial, for example, established in order to provide the means for trustworthy decisions on matters of fact, is used all too frequently for purposes of delay. Absurd motions likewise enter the picture. In the long run the actual issue comes to be laid over with a network of unessential matters of strategy.

So long as years of delay are assured by the condition of

the calendars of the courts, this delay itself will be used to threaten those who have rightful claims. Such delays constitute actual denials of justice; on the other hand, those defendants who have legitimate defenses are threatened with long and irritating legal processes. It is a common thing among courts where reform has been attempted that the very fact that justice has been made more expeditious means the quick settlement of many cases that should never have been in the courts at all. Thousands of cases find their way into the courts for the simple reason that to put them there, with the delay involved, is to set up a means to force an unjust settlement. Long delay is caused by non-meritorious cases, and non-meritorious cases are put into the courts because of long delay. The whole thing is a vicious circle.

The only way to attack the problem is by rigorous application of judicial efficiency. In the face of this congestion the remedy commonly proposed is to add new judges or new courts, but it will readily be seen that if the problem is what I have stated it to be, such a so-called remedy merely aggravates the complaint. There are, of course, legitimate demands for additional judicial manpower in sections where the population has grown rapidly. But it is easy to see that to apply this remedy in all cases is to add to the ravages of the disease, to contribute to the confusion, and, what is profoundly important at this time, to burden still further an already seriously embarrassed taxpayer. With taxes mounting in all the subdivisions of government, the time has come for a veritable searching of heart with regard to the cost of the public service, and new demands should be most carefully scrutinized in the light of this problem of dollars and cents.

Moreover, the cost to the litigant is very serious. This applies not only to the cost imposed by the governmental authorities but professional fees as well. An English lawyer, in a very discriminating statement concerning the administration of justice in his own country, recently said that justice in no country in the world is so expensive to obtain as in England, except in the United States. Writers and lawyers in Continental countries comment severely on this feature of Anglo-American government. In Germany, according to this authority, Claude Mullins, an ordinary civil action for fifty pounds can be brought for total fees on both sides of not more than eighteen pounds. On the other hand, in England and the United States the cost of litigation is still deeply embedded in the mysterious recesses of lawyers' accounts; but we may be certain that it is much, much higher. Justice, then, is not only delayed, but it is excessively costly.

Stripped of frills, the problem comes down to a question of administration. Some of the realism that goes into matters less clouded by theory and tradition needs to be applied to the administration of justice. There are, of course, important considerations of policy that distinguish the administration of justice from the administration of some of the more prosaic activities of life. But it is not too much to say that the fact that the law is a learned profession and that its exponents are men trained in theoretical wisdom and are quick to distinguish fine shades of meaning has permitted them to invest their business with an almost mystical attribute that forbids the laying of the hard hands of common sense on the things they are doing.

If the experience of England is any guide to what we may expect in the way of reform, our progress out of the present unsatisfactory condition will be slow and, I fear, painful. The day of the great law-giver is past. A modern diversified and almost incoherent society requires that reform be the result of many efforts. Cooperation among the innumerable interests requires vastly detailed and patient planning and labor. While many marked improvements have taken place in the past thirty years in connection with the administration of justice, it has been notable that altogether too many well-planned attempts at improvement have failed. If we are to succeed now it must be by widespread cooperation and unflinching labor.

One of the difficulties of the past has been that attempts at reform have concerned themselves largely with the highest courts. These courts, as the result of consistent efforts on the part of reformers and largely because of the generally splendid personnel of judges who have served in them, have been a credit to the nation. It is nevertheless true that our inferior courts have been and are vastly in need of reconstructive improvement. The great delay occasioned in some of our city tribunals, the unsatisfactory nature of justice as it is administered by justices of the peace and the unsatisfactory condition in the administration of criminal justice, all point to the necessity for serious action to provide the means of justice to the poor and the unfortunate.

In the quest of reform there is no question as to the willingness of leaders of the bar to assist not only individually as lawyers but through the various legal associations. Vast energy and sums of money have been spent in order to justify the expectation of those who believe that lawyers ought to be in the forefront of reform in this field. But in spite of the professional cooperation and assistance, I have felt from the beginning that reform cannot ultimately succeed unless it is participated in by the lay public. For example, in the creation of a Commission on the Administration of Justice for the State of New York, I insisted that there be lay membership. England found in the long struggle for legal reform in the nineteenth century that laymen were indispensable.

Kenneth Dayton, Chairman of the Committee on Law Reform of the Association of the Bar, says of the part that laymen played in law reform in England: "The lesson of the early battlers has not been lost upon the English public. Increasingly, the examination into the administration of justice and its improvement has been delegated to laymen. The first commission appointed in 1850 consisted of seven attorneys, but on petition of Parliament two business men were added to the commission. The proportion of laymen upon subsequent commissions has constantly increased. A Parliamentary committee appointed in 1909 contained but one lawyer out of ten members. The 1913 commission was made up of one judge, two lawyers and eight laymen. Of this commission it was said 'even this meager representation of the legal profession was objected to by the commission as discrediting its report.'"

The laymen are the people. They have no vested interests, except in unusual instances, in the administration of justice. They are not lawyers with the fear of antagonizing the judiciary, nor are they judges who hesitate to reconstruct the conditions under which they work. Moreover, the intelligent layman is liable to cut through cobwebs that frustrate the efforts of the lawyers.

It is now clear to all thoughtful observers that reform in the administration of justice means an attack much more fundamental than the mere alteration of the rules of procedure, though these must be altered. It is more a problem of government than of law. It is concerned with questions of administrative policy and with social welfare.

This involves a broad search of the experience of the various states and most certainly of other countries. It means that we should, wherever possible, adopt the best. For example, there has developed throughout the country a system for the management of the court calendar which originated in Cleveland and the details of which are familiar to many members of the bar. The Federal Courts in New York have adopted it and the New York State Supreme Court of the First Department are thus expediting their business and at the same time saving money for litigants and taxpayers.

Some legislation, perhaps even a number of constitutional changes within the states, is desirable, but the most important improvements can be achieved without new laws.

A thoughtful judge in the City of New York, Bernard Shientag, commenting upon the need for judicial statistics, says that "the absence of such statistics has, more than any-thing else, checked the progress of the law."

One of the activities of the State Commission I appointed is the creation throughout the State of a system by which there will be state-wide statistics concerning all of the courts. It is planned that this work should be carried on and if and when a permanent judicial council is created, the present temporary commission will divest itself of this function and transfer it to such a permanent body.

The value of such information, systematically gathered and intelligently presented, is of extraordinary importance. It will give officials themselves a picture of the state of liti-gation in the courts which will permit us to know what work the courts are doing, how much of it there is, and how long it takes to dispose of cases. It will, I hope, be a permanent guide to the legislatures in the creation of new courts and new judges. It will give us an assurance that we shall not be permitted to enact legislation adding to the expense of the courts, without accurate scientific means of knowing the extent of the need and whether it is immedi-ately necessary.

Action required in law reform may in many respects be applied with singular appropriateness to much of public life today. The principle of fewer new laws has been widely advocated; but that has too often been the cry of touchy conservatism, a wish to escape the regulatory arm of the government. The general wisdom of the demand for fewer laws is undeniable. But its necessary correlative principle is to use with intelligence and energy the powers that we have. Administration, informed, energetic and economical, is a deep need of government today. The public, particularly in these moments of stress, deserves of its servants an example of unselfish application to duty.

Every member of the bar has something of the character of a public servant and he owes it to his profession and to the public to encourage and to give his efforts for the correction of the faults in the administration of justice which I have pointed out.

XII

CRIME AND CRIMINALS

A T ALMOST ANY moment a great crime or a series of lesser ones may startle the public into feeling, as it has often before, that decency and security require a dictatorship. This is far from the case, for every scrap of authentic information from those who have been waging war against crime and criminals, night and day, reveals that there is but one way we can reduce crime. That is through a policy of prevention.

To no other institutions of learning in the world do so many postgraduates return for advanced instruction as to those "colleges of crime" which a still unenlightened civilization, in this respect, has erected for the opposite purpose—our penal institutions, state and national.

Prison statistics show that from fifty to sixty percent of those once sent to jail become habitual offenders and eventually return again. When we consider that this huge percentage represents only those persons who have been caught in the act and have been successfully prosecuted, and that we must add those who have escaped detection or who have slipped through the many holes in our creaking and antiquated machinery of justice and prosecution, we are forced to admit that, as a protection to society, the whole prison system has been miserably inadequate and ineffective. We are only beginning to realize that the overwhelming majority of our convicted criminals return to society in a short time and become again our neighbors and active members of our community.

We have assumed that the horrors of prison life, that the stigma which society brands upon every prisoner, were forcing him through sheer terror into the path of virtue on his release. That is not true. We must always have prisons. There are always those who are criminals by instinct, who must be kept from society and from injuring others because their minds are incapable of reformation, their wills too weak to keep them from lives of crime. These must be rearrested and rearrested and rearrested. Our police records are full of criminal biographies of those who have spent, since they reached adolescence, far more time in jail than out of it. For such our prisons must be maintained.

But we are finding from practical experience that the permanent reformation of the first offender is possible in far more instances than we realized. For example, in the State of Massachusetts eighty percent of those who have been placed on probation, instead of being sent to jail, have made good. In the State of New York more than twenty-five thousand are being placed on probation yearly, as our courts and our judges have become convinced of the value of the probation system in reducing crime.

In the past twenty-four years the State of New York has placed two hundred and fifty thousand on probation.

We have, unfortunately, no figures showing how many of these were permanently reformed in New York, but they have contributed in that time over twenty-three millions of dollars in fines, restitutions and support of dependents; and I have no doubt that the percentage of permanent reformations in New York State closely approximates that of Massachusetts.

There are three ways of dealing with the first offender. We can send him to jail and keep him there until the expiration of his sentence; we can parole him before the sentence expires; or we can put him on probation after he is sentenced without his going to jail at all.

Let me make clear the difference between probation and parole, for it is often confused in the public mind. When a convicted prisoner, at the time of his sentence, is released from custody but kept under the observation of a court officer, without going to prison to serve any part of his sentence, he is said to be placed on probation. If he is actually sent to prison, but later found worthy of being released, again under the observation and technically in the custody of a special officer, he is said to be placed on parole.

In both cases his past record is looked into before action is taken and a failure to report to the proper officer, or a new offense against the law, sends him to prison to serve out his sentence with added penalties.

If the criminal's past history gives good reason to believe that he is not of the naturally criminal type, that he is capable of real reform and of becoming a useful citizen, there is no doubt that probation, viewed from the selfish standpoint of protection to society alone, is the most efficient method that we have, and yet it is the least appreciated of all our efforts to rid society of the criminal.

By segregation, by removing the first offender from the demoralizing contact with the habitually criminal, by a study of the criminal himself, treating him as an individual rather than in the mass, we can do much to reduce that staggering percentage of second offenders.

By shortening the terms of those who show, after their incarceration, hopeful symptoms of a real repentance, we can add a still greater number of good citizens to our communities.

By investigation of the past history of first offenders or of those who, in the opinion of the judge who tries the case, have been the victims somewhat of circumstances and who are not hopelessly criminal in their tendencies, and by the placing of such as are found worthy upon probation, I believe we shall empty our prisons still further.

Economically, probation is to the financial advantage of the State. Statistics show that it costs, roughly, eighteen dollars a year to supervise each person released on probation. Under more watchful scrutiny and closer observation it may perhaps eventually cost as much as twenty-five dollars for each person. Against that set the three hundred and fifty to five hundred dollars a year it costs the State to keep a man in jail a year. I hope that in all states we shall be continually decreasing the number of our prison guards and wardens and increasing the number of our parole and probation officers.

Probation officers, however, must be properly trained and competent persons. In this we have been lamentably weak. We shall find a way to secure really qualified probation officers, just as we are now insisting on really competent parole officers. It is a state's affair and this whole matter of probation should be made the state's business and put under wide state control.

Probation in one form or another has been established in twenty-one out of the forty-eight states. By its intelligent extension crime can be decreased, the overcrowded conditions in our penal institutions greatly ameliorated and the necessity for building more and more prisons, for needlessly and ineffectively spending huge prison budgets, reduced.

The report of the commission which I appointed to investigate prison administration and construction in the State of New York, with Mr. Sam A. Lewisohn as chairman, reported in February, 1932, some most pertinent facts, and made some important comments. The commission told me, "If reformation is the objective, it will, in the majority of cases, be accomplished in a relatively short time. Incarceration over a long period will, of itself, unfit the individual for return to society on a useful basis, or make such a procedure exceedingly difficult, if not hopeless." I am sure the commission is right.

Their report pointed out that the indeterminate sentence law originally registered its opinion of the gravity of a crime by the length of the maximum sentence. Unfortunately amendments "during the last few years have in most instances completely destroyed or rendered impotent the spirit of the indeterminate sentence law. The long *minimum* sentences brought about by these amendments prevent the application of modern reformative measures, as it is impossible to apply them in many instances because of the likelihood of escape. As an illustration, it is frequently found that two young men have been convicted of identical offenses—one given a reformatory sentence with no minimum and the other a prison sentence the minimum of which, in some instances, has been as high as seventy years. It is obvious that there is no hope for reformation in the latter case."

I should like to give some examples of inhuman sentences which have come to my knowledge in the State of New York, through this same report. In a group of one hundred and seventy-six first offenders recently surveyed at Sing Sing Prison, the aggregate minimum sentences totalled around three thousand five hundred years and the aggregate maximum sentences between five and six thousand years.

In Auburn Prison, there are two youths, age twenty-one and twenty-five, who are serving sentences of forty-seven years and six months to life for robbery. One of these will be sixty-eight and the other seventy-two years of age when released. One man sixty-nine years of age is serving a sentence of from fifteen to thirty years for robbery. He will be eighty-four years of age when released.

In Sing Sing Prison one youth, aged twenty years, is serving a sentence of from forty-five to ninety years for robbery. He will be sixty-five years of age if released at the expiration of his minimum term. Another youth of nineteen is serving a sentence of from thirty to sixty years for robbery. A third, aged twenty-nine, is serving a sentence of twenty-five to fifty years. In Clinton Prison a boy of twenty-one is serving a sentence of from seventy to eighty years. Another, twenty, is serving a sentence fifty-seven years and six months to life. . . . But why go on?

The whole thing is a tremendous human tragedy, apart from the crimes which were tragedy enough, for these men have no chance to come back—and some of them can. From the cold practical standpoint the commission declares that such indiscriminate severity is "a very costly experiment for the State and one which may create very serious financial problems in the large increase entailed in prison capacity."

As a result of a public hearing in which Judges, District Attorneys, members of the Division of Parole of the State and others were invited to discuss this problem, the following recommendation was advanced by the commission: that a section of the Penal Law be amended to provide that in instances where it is felt that the minimum sentence imposed by the court is too severe, that the Parole Board be empowered to make application to the committing court for a re-sentence, which may result in a reduction of the original minimum sentence. When the application for a reduction of the minimum sentence is before the court the district attorney shall be entitled to be heard. Provided that the judge agrees to a reduction of the minimum sentence the offender shall then be eligible for consideration for parole subject to such conditions on release as may be lawfully imposed by the Parole Board.

It is certain that the severity of sentences has not prevented a marked increase in convictions.

The code of criminal procedure and penal law in most of the states needs a new study. There should be a new basis of criminal jurisprudence which shall seek not only to punish criminals but to restore them to society. Only then shall we really succeed in our war upon crime in this country.

XIII

Banking and Speculation

THERE HAS BEEN a terrible race between the rising tide of bubble fortunes in the stock market and unemployment. Even in 1925 there were two million fewer men at work in the principal fields of employment than there had been six years previously, although the population and production had vastly increased and many new industries had appeared. A program of buy more, owe more and spend more, caused the deluge of high-pressure selling, lavish extravagance, head-on plunges into debt and the wildest speculation the nation had ever seen. It was the heyday of promoters, sloganeers, mushroom millionaires, opportunists, adventurers of all kinds.

It was already obvious in 1928 that the forced production of our industry was far too great for our domestic markets. This fact was met by an audacious and fateful suggestion from the leaders of the national government. We were to sell "the constantly increasing surplus" abroad. But how could this be done in the collapsed state of world finance? The answer which was tragically wrong, was made: "It is an essential part of the further expansion of our foreign trade that we should interest ourselves in the development of backward or crippled countries by means of loans." I have mentioned this policy before, but it is necessary to do so again because it played so great a part in our difficulties in banking and speculation. The United States which had already loaned fourteen billions of dollars abroad was lending overseas at the rate of two billions a year. Thus was produced in fact the crop of foreign bonds which American investors know to their cost.

The old economics had gone out of business; to the suggestion that mass and machine production must ultimately destroy employment, it was simply observed that the idea was a reecho of a century before. So the new economics went merrily on. The agitation had already begun for the raising of higher protective tariffs. A copper-riveted American market was desired, sealed by the highest tariff in the history of the world. American industry, accelerated to a pace never before known, suddenly found the brakes locked on a slippery road. The law of gravity did the rest.

For some years the collapse of farm prices had prostrated agriculture, with nothing done to help. In industry, larger industrial groups, mergers, holding companies, began to return fabulous paper profits; but the number of corporations reporting net income was steadily diminishing. In banking, Paul Warburg, a great financial authority and a great man who had given years of his life to the original building up of the Federal Reserve System, issued early in 1929 public warning that speculation had gone wild and that the country would have to pay for it. Notwithstanding the appearance of prosperity, unemployment was steadily increasing. Months before, the American Federation of Labor had sounded an alarm with regard to the rapid decrease in the number of jobs.

The Federal Reserve Board saw the clouds too, but did little.

It has been suggested that the American public was apparently elected to the rôle of Alice in Wonderland; and I agree that Alice was peering into the looking glass of the new economics. White knights had great schemes of unlimited sales in foreign markets and discounted the future ten years ahead. The poorhouse was to vanish like the Cheshire cat. A Mad Hatter invited everyone to "have some more profits," though there were no profits, except on paper. A cynical Father William in the lower district of Manhattan balanced the sinuous eel on the end of his nose. A puzzled, somewhat skeptical Alice, asked some simple questions:

"Will not the printing and selling of more stocks and bonds, the building of new plants, and the increase of efficiency, produce more goods than we can buy?"

"No!" shouted Jabberwock. "The more we produce, the more we can buy."

"What if we produce a surplus?"

"Oh, we can sell it to foreign consumers."

"How can the foreigners buy it?"

"Why, we will lend them the money."

"I see," says Alice, "they will buy our surplus with our

own money. Of course, these foreigners will pay us back by sending us their goods?"

"Oh, not at all," says Humpty Dumpty. "We sit on a high wall of a Hawley-Smoot Tariff."

"How will the foreigners pay off these loans?"

"That is easy; did you ever hear of a moratorium?"

Silly as it may seem, here we are at the heart of the magic formula of 1928. This "lift yourself up by your own boot-straps" theory was believed; it appeared to work. Under the spell of this fable the people sacrificed on the altar of the stock markets the frugal savings of a lifetime. Business men sincerely believed that they had heard expert advice and risked their solvency by a new burst of expansion. Bankers made their loans not wisely but too much. Common sense was hushed before the spell of an economic necromancy.

Between August, 1928, and the end of that year the market balloon rose thirty percent. It did not stop. It went up and up for many fantastic months, until at last it was eighty percent higher than the year before. These were figures of a dream. The balloon had reached the economic stratosphere, above the air, where mere men cannot survive. Then came the crash. The paper profits vanished overnight; the savings pushed into the market at the peak, dwindled to nothing. Only the cold reality remained—the debts were real—the only realities in the cold dawn of deflation amid a nebulous welter of magnificently engraved certificates not worth the cost of the artistic scroll-work upon them.

The depression steadily deepened.

Explanations and false hopes were held out again and

again that the worst was over. Now, there was nothing more in all this than a wild gamble that the situation would, in some unexplained way, come out right. The Federal Budget for 1930 was arranged on the theory that nothing had altered. The safety of our financial system, the jobs and livings of millions of individuals and the safety of business enterprises in general, were staked on this guess. The people who faced the facts were saved; the others were ruined.

Not for partisan purposes but in order to set forth history aright it is necessary, even here, to state the facts. In October of 1931, the official policy of the national administration was: "The depression has been deepened by events from abroad which are beyond the control of either our citizens or our government." This excuse was maintained until that administration went out of power.

But the records of the civilized nations of the world prove two facts: first, that the economic structure of other nations was affected by our own tide of speculation and the curtailment of our lending helped to bring on their distress; second, that the bubble burst first in the land of its origin— the United States. The major collapse abroad followed. It was not simultaneous with ours. Moreover, further curtailment of our loans, plus the continual stagnation caused by the high tariff, continued the depression throughout international commerce. If in your mind you hesitate to believe this on the grounds that it may be actuated by political motives, then I beg you to look for yourself at any reliable index of international trade, of loans, of price trends, of interest rates, of production, of the other nations of the world.

Speculation and overproduction were encouraged through false economic policies.

The crash was minimized and the people were misled as to its gravity.

The cause was erroneously charged to the other nations of the world.

By refusing to recognize and correct evils at home which had brought forth chaos, relief was delayed and reform forgotten.

The logical question before us now is this: What steps can be taken to recognize the errors of the past? What concrete remedies have been proposed to prevent them from happening in the future?

It is first necessary to look the facts squarely in the face. They are as follows: Two-thirds of American industry is concentrated in a few hundred corporations, and actually managed by not more than five thousand men. More than half of the savings of the country are invested in corporation stocks and bonds, which have been made the sport of the American stock markets. Fewer than three dozen private banking houses, and stock-selling adjuncts in the commercial banks, have directed the flow of capital within the country and outside it. Economic power is concentrated in a few hands. A great part of our working population has no chance of earning a living except by the grace of this concentrated economic machinery. Millions of Americans are out of work, throwing upon the already overburdened government the necessity of relief. The tariff has cut off any chance of a foreign market for our products—the effect of which has been the cutting of the earnings of the farmer to the extent of threatening him generally with foreclosure and want.

In outlining my economic creed it is necessary to make clear again my point of view with regard to the individual. I believe that our industrial and economic system is made for individual men and women, and not individual men and women for the benefit of the system. I believe that the individual should have full liberty of action to make the most of himself; but I do not believe that in the name of that sacred word, individualism, a few powerful interests should be permitted to make industrial cannon-fodder of the lives of half the population of the United States. I believe in the sacredness of private property, which means that I do not believe that it should be subjected to the ruthless manipulation of professional gamblers in the stock market and in the corporate system. I share the general complaint against regimentation; I dislike it not only when it is carried out by an informal group amounting to an economic government of the United States, but also when it is done by the government of the United States itself. I believe that the government, without becoming a prying bureaucracy, can act as a check or counterbalance of this oligarchy so as to secure initiative, life, a chance to work, and the safety of savings to men and women, rather than safety of exploitation to the exploiter, safety of manipulation to the financial manipulator, safety of unlicensed power to those who would speculate to the bitter end with the welfare and property of other people.

We must get back to first principles; we must make American individualism what it was intended to be—equality of opportunity for all, the right of exploitation for none.

I propose an orderly, explicit and practical group of fundamental remedies. These will protect not the few but the great mass of average American men and women who, I am not ashamed to repeat, have been forgotten by those in power. These measures, like my own whole theory of the conduct of government, are based on telling the truth.

Government cannot prevent some individuals from making errors of judgment. But government can prevent to a very great degree the fooling of sensible people through misstatements and through the withholding of information on the part of private organizations great and small which seek to sell investments to the people.

Toward this end and to inspire truth telling, I propose that every effort be made to prevent the issue of manufactured and unnecessary securities of all kinds which are brought out merely for the purpose of enriching those who handle their sale to the public; and I further propose that with respect to legitimate securities, the sellers shall tell the uses to which the money is to be put. This truth telling requires that definite and accurate statements be made to the buyers in respect to the bonuses and commissions the sellers are to receive; and furthermore, true information as to the investment of principal, as to the true earnings, true liabilities and true assets of the corporation itself.

We are well aware of the difficulty and often the impossibility under which state governments have labored in the regulation of holding companies which sell securities in interstate commerce. It is logical and necessary that the full extent of Federal power be applied to such regulation.

We have seen the collapse of the Forshay, Ohrstrom, Insull and other lesser dynasties, and the wreck of the supposed financial safety of thousands of our citizens. The Kreuger fraud, alone, shows the urgent necessity of regulation.

For the very practical reason that the many exchanges in the business of buying and selling securities and commodities can, by the practical expedient of moving elsewhere, avoid regulation in any given state, I propose the use of Federal authority in their regulation.

The events of the past three years prove that the supervision of national banks for the protection of depositors has been ineffective. I propose much more rigid supervision.

We have witnessed not only the unrestrained use of bank deposits in speculation to the detriment of local credit but we are also aware that this speculation was encouraged by the government itself. I propose that such speculation be discouraged and prevented.

Investment banking is a legitimate business. Commercial banking is another wholly separate and distinct legitimate business. Their consolidation and mingling is contrary to public policy. I propose their separation.

Prior to the panic of 1929 the funds of the Federal Reserve System were used practically without check for many speculative purposes. I propose the restriction of Federal

Reserve Banks in accordance with the original plans and earlier practices of the Federal Reserve System.

I propose two new policies for which legislation is not required. They are policies of fair and open dealing on the part of officials of the national administration with the American, the investing, public. In the first place, I promise that it will no longer be possible for international bankers or others to sell to the investing public in America, foreign securities on the implied understanding that these securities have been passed on or approved by the State Department or any other agency of the Federal Government. I assure that high public officials in the new administration will neither by word nor deed seek to influence the prices of stocks and bonds. The government has access to vast information concerning the economic life of the country; there will be no statements at variance to the scientific information possessed.

Restored confidence in the actions and statements of executive authority is indispensable. The kind of confidence we most need is confidence in the integrity, the soundness, the liberalism, the vision and the old-fashioned horse sense of our national leadership. Without that kind of leadership we are forever insecure. With that confidence the future is ours to conquer.

XIV

HOLDING COMPANIES

THE EVILS WHICH have grown out of the holding companies must be corrected if we are to square away for a sound progress in many lines of business. The form of the holding company is inherently such that it lends itself to secrecy, mismanagement and fraud. At best the holding company is an artificial super-corporation designed to give unity of purpose and direction to more or less related businesses. There are holding companies which accomplish this purpose honestly and profitably to all concerned; but there is, unfortunately, too great a temptation to use for utterly selfish purposes the concentration of vast financial and management power they place in the hands of a few individuals.

These companies were created by ambitious financial and management interests for several purposes. They gave a broader scope to management. They facilitated intercompany sales policies and financing. They created a unity which made possible the distribution of securities. But the public often took their mere size as the illusion of integrity.

The urgent requirements of our industrial progress in the past may have justified the creation of holding companies, but gross irregularities and gigantic losses which have occurred through them demand definite control.

Within the period of our great expansion there came a change in our ways of doing business which is an important factor in the methods we shall now use to prevent the further financial exploitation of our people by the holding companies. In the past many great businesses were owned and managed by the same individuals. The matter of pride in reputation, pride in the manner of small dealings as well as the large, is just one of the many things that entered into and created the good-will of many of our older business institutions. But management, today, is not generally in the hands of ownership. Shares of corporations are owned by individuals who have never seen and never desire to see their company's office or plant and who do not possess any of the pride of ownership that used to come to a partner in a business enterprise when he watched his product, the product of his own strength and brain, moving to market. Today, controlling interests not only may have the disadvantages of absentee ownership but title may even rest in another corporation itself before it filters down into the hands of individual shareholders.

When businesses grew to such size that they were beyond individual ownership, it was not long before management became a game by which controlling interests were used as pawns. This was the logical result of the corporation method of doing business, but it added a complication which easily lent itself to the predatory designs of the unscrupulous. Businesses eventually became pawns themselves in dreams of financial empires where small stockholders no longer had any voice; it was forgotten that one individual with ten shares had as much right to demand honesty in management as another who owned five hundred or a thousand.

The size of the financial operations which developed required the use of vast capital resources, and it was at this moment that banking interests stepped in. Many unscrupulous financiers were interested primarily in the sale of securities to the public rather than in conservatively directing the affairs of the company. The more securities that were sold the greater would be their profits and so it became the plan to invent new methods and new excuses for additional flotations.

The tragedy and disillusionment today is the inevitable result of this relationship of financial and management control. Such results as we have before us today could not have occurred without collusion and a purpose which violated good morals even if not the letter of the law.

For facts, figures and definite instances of thievery, of malicious misinformation of the public, of bribery and of every sort of stock-selling abuse in connection with holding companies, the Federal Trade Commission, in its investigation of public utilities, can supply incontrovertible evidence.

Unscrupulous managers, slipping inside profits to those in on the ground floor, making illegal contracts for their own advantage rather than for that of the businesses they were paid, enormously, to manage, and receiving huge fees from operating companies for so-called services and so-called expert advice, made it their policy to conceal as much as possible of what had gone on. The falsification of accounts, the concealment of assets, the wilful confusion of a maze of inter-company agreements, the blocking of investigation by the cleverest legal devices that minds lacking in old-fashioned honor could conceive—these are but some of the abuses toward which their path took them.

What chance had the small stockholder, even though he knew what was happening? What chance had the small stockholder who believed what he was told by the cleverest promoters and spellbinders who could be employed?

Thus it was that the financial and management control of these companies wielded great power to their own advantage. If it resulted to the stockholder's disadvantage, what matter? Decent ethics of business which asked those in responsible position, "What does your conscience say in this respect?" now only whispered, "Can we get away with this without running afoul of the law?" or "How long have we before we have to cease these operations?" Indeed, personal ambition was given such freedom that the policies of these holding companies, affecting the welfare and happiness of thousands of men and women, were sometimes controlled by the most trivial personal considerations.

I have said that we must let the light in on holding companies because with complete information available to the public such irregular practices can no longer continue.

We must have uniform accounting systems.

Stockholders in holding companies, on suitable representation, must have the right at any time to examine the transcript of every word that is said at a directors' meeting.

A stockholder must have the right to examine every company contract—be it with officers or directors or with other companies.

Reports of holding companies must show actual ownership in shares and changes of ownership by officers and directors.

With the knowledge that such information can at any time become public many holding company irregularities would automatically cease.

Such simple and self-evidently necessary regulation will receive no objection from those holding companies operating to the advantage of the shareholder. The opposition which arises when legislation to this end comes under consideration will, in no small measure, furnish the investor, which is the American public, with a roster of those companies which seek to avoid the light, to avoid the controls of honesty and decency, and to continue operation under those evil conditions which have stolen the savings of many an innocent man and woman.

Government regulation of the holding companies needs to new machinery of government.

Unrestrained financial exploitations which create fictitious values never justified by earnings have been one of the great causes of our present tragic condition. Unnecessary mergers and consolidations for the purpose of exploitation have unnecessarily thrown thousands out of work. Public confidence in the men and methods employed in the use of capital is essential. We can regain that confidence by cleaning house and keeping it clean.

I should like to repeat, as I have said before, that "if we must restrict the operations of the speculator, the manipulator, even the financier, I believe that we must accept the restriction as needful, not to hamper individualism but to protect it."

Certain requirements must be satisfied, in the main, by individuals who claim and hold control of the great industrial and financial combinations which dominate so large a part of our industrial life. They have undertaken to be not business men but princes—princes of property. I am not prepared to say that the system which produces them is wrong. I am very clear that they must fearlessly and competently assume the responsibility which goes with power. So many enlightened business men know this that the statement would be little more than a platitude were it not for an added implication.

This implication is, briefly, that the responsible heads of finance and industry, instead of acting each for himself, must work together to achieve the common end.

They must, where necessary, sacrifice this or that private advantage, and in reciprocal self-denial seek a general advantage. It is here that formal government—political government, if you choose—comes in.

Whenever in the pursuit of this objective the lone wolf, the unethical competitor, the reckless promoter, the Ishmael or Insull, whose hand is against every man's, declines to join in achieving an end recognized as being for the public welfare, and threatens to drag the industry back to a state of anarchy, the government may properly be asked to supply restraint.

XV

NATIONAL AND
INTERNATIONAL UNITY

THE LONG VIEW should not be confused by items of temporary expediency. Hence I have described the entire compass of my policy as a "concert of interests"—north and south, east and west—agriculture, industry, commerce and finance. With this broad purpose in mind I have further described the spirit of my program as a "new deal," which is plain English for a changed concept of the duty and responsibility of government toward economic life. Into this general plan and actuated by this spirit I have been setting the details of the program intended to right specific troubles of specific groups without, at the same time, inflicting hardships upon other groups. Above all, my program has looked to the long view, intending to see that the factors that brought about our present condition may not occur again.

The central fact of our economic life is its failure to see beyond the barriers of immediate concerns. Perhaps it is too strong a word to call this ignorance, but it certainly means that we do not know enough about ways to produce and we do not know enough about ways to keep on producing. With the most efficient system of industry ever devised our country has been brought to the point of reducing its output by one half while most of us sit around in bewilderment and indecision. We need to know how to keep on working. If we can learn this, and I believe we can, all our other problems can be solved with ease.

The theory upon which we have been producing for years is a shocking impossibility; it is that goods can be produced that cannot be bought.

There are two unusual features which characterized business during our late decade of prosperity. First, great strides toward productive efficiency were made. Second, the goods produced by this efficiency were in large part being purchased on credit. Credit is of course a necessity to business. But today we know that our recent use of credit was ungoverned and unmeasured. To reduce it to homely terms, people incurred more debts than they could safely carry and the incurrence of this debt, encouraged as it was by reckless statements from Washington, had much to do with the crash that we experienced.

To prevent such an unmeasured expansion of credit is the task of statesmanship in the next few years. That is not to say that I favor the use of complete government control over the use of credit, but that I do propose the use of government assistance in bringing to the attention of producer and consumer alike such enlightened information as will enable the people to protect themselves against unwarranted and headlong plunges into excessive debt. It is up to the government to maintain its most sacred trust, the welfare of its citizens. And such a trust requires the regulation of such balance among productive processes as will tend to a stabilization of the structure of business. That such a balance ought to be maintained by cooperation within business itself goes without saying. It is my hope that interference of government to bring about such a stabilization can be kept at a minimum, limiting itself perhaps to a wise dissemination of information.

The other factor is that whenever income in any great group of the population becomes so disproportionate as to dry up purchasing power within any one group, the balance of economic life is thrown out of order. It is a proper concern of government to use wise measures of regulation such as will bring this purchasing power back to normal. This emergency exists among the farmers in this country today and I have not hesitated to say that the government owes a duty with respect to the restoration of their purchasing power.

Other industries have problems which are in many essentials similar to those of agriculture and they ought to be met in similar ways. Most of the other industries are more highly integrated, however, and their planning policies are frequently further advanced. I mentioned two categories of those who are suffering the worst of contemporary distresses. Besides the farmers, there are the workers in other industries.

We need for them a greater measure of security. Old-age, sickness and unemployment insurance are minimal requirements in these days. But they are not enough. Whether we are thinking of the heartbreaking problem of present distress and of the possibilities of preventing its recurrence in the future, or whether we are merely thinking about the prosperity and continuity of industry itself, we know now that some measure of regularization and planning for balance among industries, and for envisaging production as a national activity, must be devised. We must set up some new objectives; we must have new kinds of management. Business must think less of its own profit and more of the national function it performs. Each unit of it must think of itself as part of a greater whole, one piece in a larger design.

I believe with all my heart that business and professional men have a high sense of their responsibilities as American citizens and a high regard for the public welfare. I am confident that they will go along with me in working wholeheartedly toward the national good in the broadest sense of that term.

Instead of romantic adventurings in foreign markets we expect and hope to substitute realistic study and actual exchange of goods. We shall try to discover with each country in turn the things which can be exchanged with mutual benefit and shall seek to further this exchange to the best of our ability. This economic interchange is the most important item in our country's foreign policy.

Out of economic disputes arise the irritations which leap to competitive armaments and are fruitful causes of war. More realistic mutual arrangements for trade, substituted for the present system in which each nation attempts to exploit the markets of every other, giving nothing in return, will do more for the peace of the world and will contribute more to supplement the eventual reduction of armament burdens than any other policy which could be devised. And at the same time it will make possible the approach to a national economic policy at home which will have as its central feature the fitting of production programs to the actual probabilities of consumption. At least the issue will no longer be confused by the impossible hopes of selling in foreign markets which cannot now pay for their products. There will no longer be the excuse for the overbuilding of American industries. And they can begin the process of accommodation to markets on which they can count. This has been too long delayed.

The relations between government and business will necessarily be in process of redefinition during the coming years. I said in a speech which redefined individualism in modern terms that business leaders are now expected to assume the responsibilities which accompany their power. A great deal can be done in this way, especially if we mobilize public opinion.

Our new national administration is going to restore the confidence that the majority of men and women in this country rightfully repose in their own integrity and ability. It is going to bring about governmental action to mesh more with the rights and the essential needs of the individual man and woman.

These are not merely hopes. These are the battle-orders

imposed upon myself and my party. I began and ended the Presidential campaign along those lines. I am going to begin our new national administration upon them.

I have forgiven the personalities of the heat of the campaign. I do not forget that many fine men were forced out of office by the election. They were so fettered by old-fashioned political commitments and strait-jacketed by outworn policies that they were literally bound hand and foot. But we must never forget the harm of these commitments and the anachronism of these policies. We must remember them well in order to recognize their faults and avoid the creation of similar ones for the future.

Our new national administration has already faced the facts in its economic campaign attacks upon our major problems. It is going to tell the truth about current conditions and their relation to the future. Perhaps of all, the first great truth is with regard to a general condition and we must face it at once. Emergency relief under way and planned will succeed only in the vital work of maintaining life. But it corrects nothing. From now on we must be far more concerned with the quality of life itself. Concentration upon purely temporary relief measures must not cause a "freezing" of national progress along lines of social equality and justice. If our present social order is to endure, it must prove itself worthy of our toil and self-sacrifice and of the lives of those who have been before us. And it must prove itself worthy within the next few years.

We must recognize that there have been profound changes in the economic forces of the world in a very short period. We must also understand those changes, comparatively slow in coming, which impose a new set of actualities upon us. There is nothing new in saying that we are now the creditor nation of the world, but our people have not yet realized its implications. Capital for our expansion into the West came from abroad. It was not until the early eighteen nineties that foreign financing became unnecessary. At the time of the World War the tide changed because of the pressing needs of Europe. Our participation in the expansion of international industry is too recent to require comment, though we know by bitter experience that some of it was unwise. The economic depression greatly jeopardized the security of all loans. The inability of some of our creditors to pay should bring home to us the radical nature of the change in international affairs. It would be well for some of our professional critics to remember that in our form of government we are now one of the older nations of the world, through our most severe political growing pains, arrived at mature years and with a new sense of responsibility toward the rest of the world.

That is why what was loaned by our people through their government must be repaid by foreign governments to our people. It is sound common sense to assist your debtors in every way, but there is neither practicality nor honor nor world safety in cancellation. The stabilization of world finance can best be achieved by a clear understanding of just obligations. A policy unduly favoring foreign loans has resulted in more great sums being owed us, has failed to achieve any real international unity, and has confirmed foreign hopes for a repudiation of debts. Our new administration will deal fairly, honestly and sanely with this situation. It will remember, however, that as society is now organized, we are divided into nations and that it is the duty of our administration to first consider the welfare of its own people. I strongly feel that the welfare of the world depends just as much upon ourselves as it does upon others, but there is only one view to be taken of these great money obligations between nations. These sums represent national labor, the labor of a great mass of individuals.

Any haziness with regard to our international position upon debts is as dangerous as that which has led us into serious social injustices within the past few years. I refer to the fact that a haziness with regard to just and unjust monopolies has been fostered within recent years, resulting in an aggressive encroachment of the desires of the few upon the rights of the many. The few have rights which must be preserved; at the same time the human rights of the many are paramount.

We must ask what an administration can do to improve the quality of life in this nation. We must decide, and the administration must see eye to eye with us, upon that factor in the national life which can best be used to make events move. We must support with aggressive vigor every effort along that line and encourage its momentum. It should be the foundation of the administrative policy. It should underlie all plans on detailed issues. What is this single factor in the United States and the world today?

It is interdependence—our mutual dependence one upon

the other—of individuals, of businesses, of industries, of towns, of villages, of cities, of states, of nations. Thorough understanding of and the proper use of interdependence is vital—first, to get a clear view of our problems, second, to really solve them.

The problems and the policies of our new national administration show the fact of this interdependence—the tariff, for example, being a part of every major problem. Specific action can and shall be taken to make interdependence the means for national recovery and stability.

There is no better illustration of the fact of interdependence and what may be accomplished through a real understanding of it than in the recent personal experience of countless families in every part of this country today. These families, supported by agricultural or industrial labor, through no fault of their own have found themselves in physical want, in privation, in discouragement, in fear. Business men who have been successful through honesty, hard work and the fruits of experience, have had their "safe investments" swept away in addition to the loss of their jobs. Yet when these families faced facts, they discovered anew that the vital factor for self-preservation and any possible progress was the dependence of one upon the other. This realization spurred each member of the family to the full performance of his duty to every other member. Thus courage was restored and forward-looking plans developed.

Human interdependence is no more true than economic interdependence. Our economic problems, however, are simplified, rather than complicated by their interdependence and the fact that economic laws are definitely man made. I should like to repeat in practically the same words as my acceptance speech:

"Never in history have the interests of all the people been so united in a single economic problem. Picture to yourself the groups of property represented in the form of bonds and mortgages—government bonds of all kinds, bonds of industrial and utility companies, mortgages on real estate and the vast investments of the nation in the railroads. Each and every one of them affects the whole financial fabric. . . ."

My responsibility will be to direct relief toward all these groups together. I shall prevent efforts which would give one favored group priority over another. In this connection, the easing of the burden of taxation is a work which can be accomplished through a thorough understanding of interdependence. The whole field, as I have said before, of the sources of taxation should be allotted between the Federal and the State governments in order to do away with the present unjust duplication.

The general understanding of interdependence has grown almost in direct ratio to the decline of personal security in the last four years. Whether the result is called fraternity, or mutual responsibility, or the understanding of social justice, makes little difference. Out of this growth I see a closer meshing of every line of human endeavor and a greater unity for this nation.

As the different parts of our territories come steadily nearer by reason of time-saving devices of modern communication and travel, each man and woman becomes more and more responsible for the human conditions surrounding all of his or her nearer and nearer neighbors. It is the same with nations.

At the risk of repeating, for the sake of clarity, several things which have been noted before, it is obvious that many of our international problems are also interdependent with each other.

For example, success in a practical program limiting armaments, abolishing certain instruments of warfare and decreasing the offensive of attacking power of all nations will, in my judgment, have a very positive and salutary influence on debt and economic discussions.

As to economic conferences, I am clear that an economic program for the world should not be submerged in conversations relating to disarmament or to debts. I recognize, of course, a relationship, but not an identity. Therefore, I cannot go along with the thought that the personnel conducting the conversations should be identical. These arrangements will be found to require selective treatment, even though this be with full recognition of the possibility that in the ultimate outcome a relationship may become clear.

I have good reason to believe that many nations who, like us, are suffering from the stoppage of industry, will meet us halfway and put all the cards on the table for the purpose of breaking an actual deadlock which has paralyzed world trade and thrown millions here and abroad out of useful work. Let me at the same time make it clear that a trade conference with the other nations of the world does not, and should not, involve the United States in any participation in political controversies in Europe or elsewhere. Nor does it involve the renewal in any way of the problem of twelve years ago of American participation as a member of the League of Nations.

In common with millions of my fellow countrymen, I worked and spoke, in 1920, in behalf of American participation in a League of Nations, conceived in the highest spirit of world friendship for the great object of preventing a return of world war. For that course I have no apology to make.

If, today, I believed that the same or even similar factors entered into the argument, I would still favor America's entry into the League; and I would go so far as to seek to win over the overwhelming opposition which exists in this country today. But the League of Nations today is not the League of Nations conceived by Woodrow Wilson. It might have been had the United States joined. Too often through these years its major function has been not the broad overwhelming purpose of world peace but rather a mere meeting place for the political discussion of strictly European political national difficulties. In these the United States should have no part.

American participation in the League would not serve the highest purpose of the prevention of war and a settlement of international difficulties in accordance with fundamental American ideals; the League has not developed through these years along the course contemplated by its founder, nor have the principal members shown a disposition to divert the huge loans spent on armaments into the channels of legitimate trade, balanced budgets and payment of obligations.

The difficulties with regard to these obligations can be measurably obviated, I am convinced, if we are realistic about providing ways and means in which payment is possible through the profits rising from the rehabilitation of trade by tariff adjustments.

The depression has opened the eyes of many men to their social responsibilities. It has opened the eyes of many politicians to their true political responsibilities to the nation. I have little personal patience with those men—Democrats and Republicans alike—who have been thinking so long in the outworn partisan grooves that they cannot see the merit of accomplishment unless it bears the label of their own party. I shall give credit where credit is due, even in the camp of my partisan enemies. To this extent I shall personally erase partisan lines.

Some of the most practical, hard-headed and ambitious men I know have been so buffeted by circumstances these last few years that they realize they must all get down on their knees together in a new humbleness of spirit—out of which grows united and effective action.

I shall repeat many times that I shall ceaselessly endeavor to bring government back to a more intimate understanding of and relation to human problems. This is essential, that government may serve the basic purpose for which it was originally created.

The American people have been thoroughly disillusioned

concerning our economic policies at home and abroad. There has arisen an insistent demand for a new deal. I have been telling you some of the ways in which I conceive these insistent demands ought to be met. I should like to say again that there is neither magic nor cure-all in any of this. Hard necessity drives us now. The mandate is clear and peremptory. These are the things we must do. They are methods to be tried for attaining a genuine concert of interests. I desire to pledge myself to this service. It will be long and arduous; with the help of all of you we shall reach the goal. I look forward with confidence.

XVI

INAUGURAL ADDRESS

(Delivered at Washington, March 4th, 1933)

THIS IS A day of national consecration, and I am certain that on this day my fellow Americans expect that on my induction into the Presidency I will address them with a candor and a decision which the present situation of our people impels.

This is pre-eminently the time to speak the truth, the whole truth, frankly and boldly. Nor need we shrink from honestly facing conditions in our country today. This great nation will endure as it has endured, will revive and will prosper. So first of all let me assert my firm belief that the only thing we have to fear is fear itself—nameless, unreasoning, unjustified terror which paralyzes needed efforts to convert retreat into advance.

In every dark hour of our national life a leadership of frankness and of vigor has met with that understanding and support of the people themselves which is essential to victory, and I am convinced that you will again give that support to leadership in these critical days.

In such a spirit on my part and on yours, we face our

common difficulties. They concern, thank God, only material things. Values have shrunk to fantastic levels; taxes have risen; our ability to pay has fallen; government of all kinds is faced by serious curtailment of income; the means of exchange are frozen in the currents of trade; the withered leaves of industrial enterprise lie on every side; farmers find no markets for their produce, and the savings of many years in thousands of families are gone.

More important, a host of unemployed citizens face the grim problem of existence, and an equally great number toil with little return. Only a foolish optimist can deny the dark realities of the moment.

And yet our distress comes from no failure of substance. We are stricken by no plague of locusts. Compared with the perils which our forefathers conquered because they believed and were not afraid, we have still much to be thankful for. Nature still offers her bounty, and human efforts have multiplied it. Plenty is at our doorstep, but a generous use of it languishes in the very sight of the supply.

Primarily, this is because the rulers of the exchange of mankind's goods have failed through their own stubbornness and their own incompetence, have admitted their failure and have abdicated. Practices of the unscrupulous money changers stand indicted in the court of public opinion, rejected by the hearts and minds of men.

True, they have tried, but their efforts have been cast in the pattern of an outworn tradition. Faced by failure of credit, they have proposed only the lending of more money. Stripped of the lure of profit by which to induce our people to follow their false leadership, they have resorted to exhortations, pleading tearfully for restored confidence. They know only the rules of a generation of self-seekers. They have no vision, and when there is no vision the people perish.

Yes, the money changers have fled from their high seats in the temple of our civilization. We may now restore that temple to the ancient truths. The measure of the restoration lies in the extent to which we apply social values more noble than mere monetary profit.

Happiness lies not in the mere possession of money; it lies in the joy of achievement, in the thrill of creative effort. The joy and moral stimulation of work no longer must be forgotten in the mad chase of evanescent profits. These dark days will be worth all they cost us if they teach us that our true destiny is not to be ministered unto but to minister to ourselves and to our fellow men.

Recognition of the falsity of material wealth as the standard of success goes hand in hand with the abandonment of the false belief that public office and high political position are to be valued only by the standards of pride of place and personal profit; and there must be an end to a conduct in banking and in business which too often has given to a sacred trust the likeness of callous and selfish wrongdoing. Small wonder that confidence languishes, for it thrives only on honesty, on honor, on the sacredness of obligations, on faithful protection and on unselfish performance. Without them it cannot live.

Restoration calls, however, not for changes in ethics alone.

This nation asks for action, and action now. Our greatest primary task is to put people to work. This is no unsolvable problem if we face it wisely and courageously. It can be accomplished in part by direct recruiting by the government itself, treating the task as we would treat the emergency of a war, but at the same time through this employment accomplishing greatly needed projects to stimulate and reorganize the use of our great national resources.

Hand in hand with this we must frankly recognize the overbalance of population in our industrial centers and, by engaging on a national scale in a redistribution, endeavor to provide a better use of the land for those best fitted for the land. Yes, the task can be helped by definite efforts to raise the values of agricultural products and with this the power to purchase the output of our cities. It can be helped by preventing realistically the tragedy of the growing loss, through foreclosure, of our small homes and our farms. It can be helped by insistence that the Federal, state and the local governments act forthwith on the demand that their cost be drastically reduced. It can be helped by the unifying of relief activities which today are often scattered, uneconomical and unequal. It can be helped by national planning for and supervision of all forms of transportation and of communications and other utilities which have a definitely public character. There are many ways in which it can be helped, but it can never be helped by merely talking about it. We must act; we must act quickly.

And, finally, in our progress toward a resumption of

work, we require two safeguards against a return of the evils of the old order; there must be a strict supervision of all banking and credits and investments; there must be an end to speculation with other people's money; and there must be provision for an adequate but sound currency. . . .

Through this program of action we address ourselves to putting our own national house in order and making income balance outgo. Our international trade relations, though vastly important, are in point of time and necessity secondary to the establishment of a sound national economy. I favor as a practical policy the putting of first things first. I shall spare no effort to restore world trade by international economic readjustment, but the emergency at home cannot wait on that accomplishment.

The basic thought that guides these specific means of national recovery is not narrowly nationalistic. It is the insistence, as a first consideration, upon the interdependence of the various elements in and parts of the United States of America—a recognition of the old and permanently important manifestation of the American spirit of the pioneer. It is the way to recovery. It is the immediate way. It is the strongest assurance that recovery will endure.

In the field of world policy I would dedicate this nation to the policy of the good neighbor—the neighbor who resolutely respects himself and, because he does so, respects the rights of others—the neighbor who respects the sanctity of his agreements in and with a world of neighbors.

If I read the temper of our people correctly, we now realize as we have never realized before our interdependence on each other; that we cannot merely take, but we must give as well; that, if we are to go forward, we must move as a trained and loyal army willing to sacrifice for the good of a common discipline, because without such discipline no progress can be made, no leadership become effective. We are, I know, ready and willing to submit our lives and our property to such discipline because it makes possible a leadership which aims at the larger good. This I propose to offer, pledging that the larger purposes will bind upon us, bind upon us all as a sacred obligation with a unity of duty hitherto evoked only in time of armed strife. With this pledge taken, I assume unhesitatingly the leadership of this great army of our people, dedicated to a disciplined attack upon our common problems.

Action in this image, action to this end is feasible under the form of government which we have inherited from our ancestors. Our Constitution is so simple and practical that it is possible always to meet extraordinary needs by changes in emphasis and arrangement without loss of essential form. That is why our constitutional system has proved itself the most superbly enduring political mechanism the modern world has ever seen. It has met every stress of vast expansion of territory, of foreign wars, of bitter internal strife, of world relations.

And it is to be hoped that the normal balance of executive and legislative authority may be wholly equal, wholly adequate to meet the unprecedented task before us. But it may be that an unprecedented demand and need for un-delayed action may call for temporary departure from that normal balance of public procedure.

I am prepared under my constitutional duty to recommend the measures that a stricken nation in the midst of a stricken world may require. These measures, or such other measures as the Congress may build out of its experience and wisdom, I shall seek, within my constitutional authority, to bring to speedy adoption.

But in the event that the Congress shall fail to take one of these two courses, in the event that the national emergency is still critical, I shall not evade the clear course of duty that will then confront me. I shall ask the Congress for the one remaining instrument to meet the crisis—broad executive power to wage a war against the emergency, as great as the power that would be given to me if we were in fact invaded by a foreign foe.

For the trust reposed in me I will return the courage and the devotion that befit the time. I can do no less.

We face the arduous days that lie before us in the warm courage of national unity; with the clear consciousness of seeking old and precious moral values; with the clean satisfaction that comes from the stern performance of duty by old and young alike. We aim at the assurance of a rounded, a permanent national life.

We do not distrust the future of essential democracy. The people of the United States have not failed. In their need they have registered a mandate that they want direct, vigorous action. They have asked for discipline and direction under leadership. They have made me the present instrument of their wishes. In the spirit of the gift, I take it.

In this dedication of a nation we humbly ask the blessing of God. May He protect each and every one of us. May He guide me in the days to come.

INDEX